Arthur Dies

Second Chronicle:

Arthur& morgAnna Ascendant

VOL. I

Being the Opening Volume of the Second Chronicle:

the s'Word & the s'Tone

*The **Sixth** Tome of the Series Entire*

OLCHAR E. LINDSANN

LBP
2024
LUNA BISONTE PRODS

ARTHUR DIES Second Chronicle Vol. 1
Arthur & morgAnna Ascendant

A portion of Chapter III was first published in *Otoliths* #67.

"The laydie of the Lesened Lake" & another portion of Chapter III were first published in *Otoliths* #70.

Portions of the Invocation, Chapters I & III, and "The laydie of the Lesened Lake" were performed on June 23, 2023 at the AfterMAF Anti-Festival in Roanoke, Virginia.

Book design and cover collage by C. Mehrl Bennett
Main image by Howard Pyle

ISBN 9781938521997

LUNA BISONTE PRODS
137 Leland Ave.
Columbus, OH 43214 USA

http://www.lulu.com/spotlight/lunabisonteprods

Table

the Second Chronicle is dedicated

to **Iván Arguëlles**

: orphic bard of our

age of shadow bearer

of balm and pharmikon for

capricious wild calliope , we

burn that torch strewn acolytes

: griot swept by mytheme sherd , seared

torch in palm aloft , the other

strumming tortoise shell with

shoe-strung lyre

: one of our epoch's twin

lungs , dream breathes

into our epic anew subliminal

your mosaic of *that*

goddess waits in shadow

with all the other halves of you go

forth , blind as the prophets .

Morgana is her name, and she has learned what useful properties all the herbs contain, so that she can cure s ick bodies. She also knows an art by which to change h er shape, and to cleave the air on new wings like Dæda lus; when she wishes"

-Geoffrey of Monmouth, *Vita Merlini.*

So said Merlin, the magus renowned,
that a king should come of Uthere Pendragune,
that bards should build a table from that king's breast,
and thereto be seated most skilful scops
and munch there til full ere rushing off,
and winegulps draw from this king's tongue,
and drink and carouse days and nights;
this game should gratify them all this world long.

– Layamon, *Brut.*

In'voca tion
for the Second Chronicle

~~~~~~~~~~~~~~~~~~~~~~~~~~~~~~~~~~~~~

"HERE we shall write,
We shall plant ancient word,
Its planting,
Its root beginning as well"
– *Popol Vuh.*

~ ~ ~

"Awake! awake O sleeper of the land of shadows, wake! expand!
I am in you and you in me, mutual in love divine:
Fibres of love from man to man thro Albion's pleas"
– Blake, *Jerusalem*, Chapt. 1, Plate 4.

~~~~~~~~~~~~~~~~~~~~~~~~~~~~~~~~~~~~~

Ô sphea*r*k
ô æolian muse'c
s,peak atop ages' eddi
faces ,ô anima nesir sun,
ô fles-ro,rrim'I stare, ô
suoetuæb diÔv ô txet
text ô vÔid beauteous
ô ,erats I'mirr,or-self ô
,nus risen amina ô, secaf
idde 'sega pota kæp,s
c'esum nialoæ ô
k*r*æ*h*ps Ô

Ô

! Da'oughters of Beulah
d/aughters thrice-de,light'd
thrice-gated sistren
in,spirant be   mine Poesy
song melodantly me/asurèd
s'urge song vib*rant* wordseeds forth
for the *pen-Dragons*
t,win'd:

Ô dea*Thoth* ink'eye

hermetic *thrice*-greated
thrice-writ hierophanaut
let word'beams yr love   dictate=>me
fix dans runic letterforms ever @ fond dialectic:
let prophememorcy yr   deascend
nerve-th*reads* from the heavens silent t'witching
in lettral rhythms @ my hand
fleshy dancing spider stroke   nimble pon the Keys
fireye brain furnace fierce sala,*man*der maned
crystal c/ave*nium's* hollow
-g,raphic d'*Anna* :death'less:

Ôrpheus of liyare mellifluent

lyreic poet *thrice*-belovèd
thrice-dead thy voices
im-pulse y*ou*r passionage via phonemic
the g/*ore*ious Deathhaul of *Arthur*   death-doomèd:

:Chronicall ici via me eht struggles et triumphs

thru Perilous Wealds of lustremoon et terror

of *Arthur* of *Anna*

of Albion=Otherway

of *Arthur* ascendant

of *Anna* ascendant

of Albion ascendant

for Avalon descends

for *Anna*+*Arther*

from Avalon desc*end*

Ô theme of m'*awe*aken

o' years m'eachen ever

,morn aft each gloamingtide

noir of waters sable

gloamingtide aft each morn

: such my theme of *Arthur* awakened

, astir ,*Anna* of theme my so :

scend ,Ô *Arthur* yrselven: mynne *tongue*

'syr sail to billowflap! mynne *vocal*
-*cords* haul 'pon like hawsers thee! mynne *vellum*
steer thee yr rudder! mynne *teeth*
tack & jibe yr consonants! ô *Arthur*
helm our poem d' Albion
to harb*ours* un*thought*!

scend ,Ô *morgAnna* yrselven: mynne *purplections*

leaden yr primateria! mynne *shadow*
yr quickend silver! mynne *jouissance*
yr flâme of quickning! mynne *t'errors*
ashed in your retort enwombed! ô *morgAnna*
trans*mute* our poem d' Albion,
re-Lapis thee our thought!

scend ,Ô *Merlin* yrselven: mynne *lines*

yr *sorc*erer's circles! mynne *verbe*
yr e*last*ic spell! mynne *syntaxe*
casteth yr magic! mynne *typynge*
t'en-sigil yr will! ô *Merlin*
evoke our poem d'Albion
too wonderliche e'er for eht paltry-thought-possible!

scend ,Ô *Lady of Lakes!*   mynne *nerves*

        yr murkish deeps!   mynne *brain*
yr em-*b*racing banks!   mynne=*mnemnory*
yr limpidlucent wavegleams!   mynne n *ever ~~self~~*
be-flowid aptability!   ô *Lady of Lakes*!
    renewrish our poem d Albion
    en re-formish -fleck our thought!

!& so many Ôthers & so many Ôthers!

from criminal Egg mundane

futurity hatches   nourishd ill
pon hinter-time's sulfur yolk
    ;wh'erefore   let us mind us
of those perished generations
    ;wh'erefore let us ever
    withinward g*host*ly gaze
    t'heir lineameants upon
quick as silver mirror skin
    ;wh'erefore let us scry them
    while propheseasons cycle
    re-member those dis-memberd
=>wh'erefore the lore of the severed tribes=> ever re-Call*!*
=>wh'erefore the loves of generation=> ever re-Call*!*
=>wh'erefore the wars of the sons of constantine=> ever re-Call*!*
=>wh'erefore the words of the dustblown fallen=> ever re-Call*!*
=>wh'erefore the crimes of rome & to*wr*=> ever re-Call*!*
=>wh'erefore the lives of the ever-dead=> ever re-Call*!*
    howe'er hence unspoke ever...

=>*wth*'ere'forget-not **W**hat

tis in five Chronicles in Crypted:

=>wh'ereforget- N ot

crastic rome of th'Real

bicephalous lycanthropempyre d'ire

fascyst ghostgrowth us haunte st'ill!

=>wh'ereforget-not

maximian-lure-pierced

falsey-footed ,bolde-r'ash

-king of vanishd arms

whoso arms her with dice her

blade grasps herselven

=>wh'ereforget- N ot

ô graithèd Albion

first-planted pen-Dragons

in the *Chaos* egg formed

in the chaos *Egg* born

constantine-pen-Dragon

glasskin coheretor -king

the deadlyest venom

:*villages for veins*

& vivienne-pen-Dragon

Lake-rebirthèd que'en

wombwater lunar

laps newborn sages

=>wh'ereforget-not

eht sunderd tribes

ye Pictes & ye Gæls

split us-from

:par Roman wayes

branched brethren

woe-cleft!

=>wh'ereforget-Not

cringelie-king vortigern
Fear-Merchant-Fearful, for-gilten
walkd in the Cloud
dperceived in the Cloud
Craven-Puppet-Pontiff
eht pavilion of fright
elopes w/ill winds
=>wh'ereforget-not
hængist hetel Horror-lord Sæxan
vortigern's bosomfriendemy
the deadlyest venom
villages for veins
Web-T*app*ing-Spyder
Net-Scanning-S'talker
Matre-Thane-Predaitor
Parch-Throat for Sangwine
,nor-for get-eht *knive-teeth'd Sæx*
Po*wr*-of-Peel'd-Pelt
Furtive-Raz*or*whip-Police
whoso arms her with terror her
blade grasps herselven
=>wh'ereforget-not
hørsa Bather-in-Brython-Blood
vortigerns bosomfriendemy Ængalish
Fierce-Frontier-Burner
Fficient-Soilblood-Settler
,nor-for get-eht *thoughtless Ængals*
Cleansed-K*ill*yng-Drones
Chanical-Gælpicte-Slayers
Death eht porcupine
rolleth in play
=>wh'ereforget-not
eht Panop-*Towr*-Hedgemon

eht pavilion of fright
elopes w/ill winds
erection of all these ,this
erection of <u>vortigern</u>, Albion doomingled
erection of <u>hængist</u>,
erection of <u>hørsa</u>,
Ængalo-Sæx *erection*
erection of Albion's shame!

yet =>wh'ereforget-N ot either

Albions resist*d*ance!
*C*re*owd*sourceful To*w*r-Bane
,nor-for get-eht
Hartfaine-Fleeting-<u>blaise</u>
,nor-for get-eht
<u>taliesin</u>-breezelippd
,nor eht his *Beacon-Sire'n-Head*
sings today
atop that henge of stone
Taliesins Beacon-Sire'n-Head
Avalon's wind w/-sings
t'Albions earen t'-songs
ribbands àdance
laugh avec chance
=>wh'ereforget-not
rightious eht pen-Dragons
they *vortigern* ~~pen-Dragon~~ *re-sisted*
they *vortigern* ~~pen-Dragon~~ *un-dragon'd*
they *vortigern* ~~pen-Dragon~~ *re-jected*
they *vortigern* ~~pen-Dragon~~ *un-pen'd*
=>wh'ereforget-not
<u>vivienne</u> violence violed fordrove
Magic-Lentless-M*o*ther
Egav*l*as-Child-Tender

=>wh'ereforget-not

ambrosius-merlinus
Son-of-Cr*ys*tal-Shaman-Sold/er
Son-of-Love-Un~~flag~~able-Que'en
sp,lit in ever scission self
de-selvd en Cr*ys*tal Cave de-*vide*d
wombwater lunar
laps newborn sages

=>wh'ereforget-not

burlish uther brash
the bawling-wolf sups on stringy wind
Fiersome-Wolf-Tail-C'law-Lord
Ram-C'razed-in-Heat-king
Arthur-St*r*eam
Anna-Foun*d*tain

=>wh'ereforget-not

w/in Armoricas bouwers
w/in Benoics'eulb arbours
refuge seeking et
refuge seeing
refuge w/sea-king
bans folk Real-bitten
th'ere Albions re-birth
conc/eiving!

=>wh'ereforget-Not

endelesse friendes
laïd out hys Ways
for *Arthur*
endelesse friendes
laïd out hyr Ways
for *Anna*

=>wh'ereforget-not
ban'dyng w/Armorican *Riothamus*
fleet of sea-foot sure
Gender-Crafting-Ocean-Fox
=>wh'ereforget-not
bold Gorrish *Uriens* Blood-Bonder
termined *Rovænna* Gang~~reine~~-Root-Severer
combatried comrades
=>wh'ereforget-not
d'alliance w/ygraine-Craggy-Bountiful
wombwater lunar
Arthur-Soil
Anna-Lake
w/gorlois-th'Ill-Fa/t/ed
the deadlyest venom
Cærnish womyn ill-rep/*aid*
=>wh'ereforget-not
dragon gargantuan skyarch har*binge*r
pen-Dragons re-turning
Albion re-nascent
,nor-for get-eht
woesome brasting battles
re-pasts pour ravnous ravens
the deadlyest venom
villages for veins
Death eht porcupine
rolleth in play
=>wh'ereforget-not
a To*w*r's Civ,ill-Licking-F,l'~~âmes~~
phalans'tries Freeflung-Loveburst-Chains
Albion Hate-shrived   green pour liberty!

et =>wh'ereforget-Not

ambrosius poison-putre*fan**ct*
pen-Dragon slain   of Stone-Giant-Helm
yet =>wh'ereforget-not either
Insect-Eyen-Masked-*Merlin*
resprouted of ambrosius-loam
Magus-re-Venant-Ph*eon*ix
wombwater lunar
laps newre~~born~~ s'ages
=>wh'ereforget-not
Albion leagued avec Gæland
beleag*uerre*d Gæland aided
ex-Eirelonde-tended en amity
=>wh'ereforget-not
camelots foundesignd in'fancy
eutopia to-commen
by ambrosius to-setten
by uther laid
mis-mid-wifen by *Merlin*

=>wh'ereforget-Not

Albion *bound*
Albion *bounteous*
Albion *beauteous*
rejouicing Albion
rejeuvant Albion
regenerantious Albion
Albion *creatuous*
Albion *commutual*
Albion *comming-led!*
=>wh'ereforget-not
fork-lintongued uther
whoso arms her with deceit her
blade grasps herselven

the bawling-wolf sups on stringy wind
uther Moc-king'bird-of-Salt
he of death-self-dealt
walked in the Cloud
saw in the Cloud
& *Arthur* seedead by hym deapth
& *Anna* ovied by hyr deapth
eht pavilion of deinception
e'lopes w/ill winds
ygraines fl'âme-blaze'doubt
Bloodew-Nursing-Pelican
she of self-death-dealt
she of matral sacriface
wombwater lunar
laps newborn sages
=>wh'ereforget-not
ygraines rattledeath-decree:
a S'tone from Albions loam
'pon a S'tone an'Anveil
in an'Anveil a S'word
in a S'word Avalons lightstrike
steel singer sœver*eign*
Arthur the S'word awaiteth
Arthur th'Anveil addresse
Arthur the S'tone acknowledges onlie!
=>wh'ereforget-not
all that chronicall dead
sad compost for *Anna*
all that chronicall dead
sad compost for *Arthur*
=>!wh'ereforget-not!
!tho we speak of't no more!

ô letten me sing may i write of *Anna* of *Arthur!*
from g'rim violation
sp,rung-let of hope be
walks in the Cloud
sees in the Cloud
s'word-girdled irony
di'spell-girded f'ires

ô letten me sing may i write of *Arthur of Anna!*
bonders ye brethren
splicers ye sistren
aye autrephillic
aye mere-assimilaphobic
ô Albion, ne:
nary fencely b'order buildeth
nary deathly b*ore*dom bolster
nor to State'ly sciencecraft bow
nor to nature's Nation buckle
:pas, ô Albion

ô letten me sing may i wRite of *Anna* of *Arthur!*
wrest Should-be What-is *from*
wrest Could-be What-is *from*
wrest Wont-be What-is *from*
wrest Cant-be What-is *from*
de-vise what cannot be
make ~~be~~ what cannot be
d'reams on die waking
eht pavilion of hope
elopes w/ill winds
yet dream-decay cyclant re-
dreamèd tis Avalons hope
tis Avalons bulb of perennial ch'urn
wombwater lunar
laps newborn sages

ô letten me sing may i wRite of *Arthur of Anna!*

t'win pla*nets* d'Albion
t'win mag*nets* t'Avalon
rêveurs of *camelot*
of *camelot* devisers
artisans of *camelot*
of *camelot* nuturemancers
twin *camelot* parents
thy gloreous riarchs
ô *camelot*-to-come
camelot countree u*nkn*own
camelot realm u*nkn*owable
camelot questscape u*nkn*owing
camelot citee of poetry
camelot epoch for poesy
camelot community in poesis
ô dual *camelot* in chronicle in dream
ô dual *camelot* of warbirth of peacedream
ô dual *camelot* in Albion in Avalon
camelot haollowèd glu*de*w
Arthur avatar
Anna avatar

ô letten me sing may i write of *Anna* of *Arthur!*

Ô

!bèmba!

! awake *Anna* waken **!**

!*Arthur* awaken *Arthur*!
!too late for us born!
!too soon away borne!
!too short ye we knew!
!too long have ye hid!
!thy mothers call you!
!yr sisters call thee!
!thy fathers call you!
!yr brothers call thee!
!thy daughters call you!
!yr sons call thee!
!Albion calls you!
!Avalon calls thee!
!*Arthur* no god heads *Anna*!

!BIRIBIRIBA!

Arthur green lyon glaren
Anna emblem*astre star*en
from death to death lives *Arthur* ne'er shall live in death
from shades to shades lives *morg**Anna* ne'er by life shall live
relict of thoughtgloom *Anna*
relict of thoughtdoom *Arthur*
Arthur reaper of hopeb'loom
Anna truthmirr'or terrible
keeper of hopendust *Anna*
thrillsome venture-hub *Arthur*
Arthur biribiriba
Anna biribiriba
wôeslayer grimliche *Arthur*
unwindswept deemstress *Anna*
Arthur ætheleste -~~king~~
\of who think mais exist not

\shedding hys tyrant-husk

Anna ætherest ~~que'en~~

\of who think mais exist not

\shattring hyr maidenshell

spark eyen *Arthur*

gleam eyen *Anna*

morg*Anna* th'*imp,*ending zephyr

!BIRIBIRIBA!

Arthur -king once

future -king *Arthur*

powers'well unseen morg*Anna*

Anna borne from death

Arthur borne for death

Arthur n'ever dead

Anna ever dead

steward of keenish elbidercni *Arthur*

surconceivably guardener *Anna*

solar *Arthur* champion of deadreams

lunar morg*Anna* slainhope-nec,romancer

Arthur dead as you shall die

Anna dead as i shall die

! hwæt !

Avalon sp'ark:

Ô

s'tuck in

*Anna***s'tone** –

t'rust in

*Arthur***s'word**

!

I

~~~~~~~~~~~~~~~~~~~~~~~~~~~~~~~~~~~~~

"ease in their misery; others, clinging to their homela
nd, eked out a wretched and fearful existence among
the mountains, forests, and crags, ever alert for dang"
–Bede, *History*, Chapt. 15.

~~~~~~~~~~~~~~~~~~~~~~~~~~~~~~~~~~~~~

Albion's state is dreadful fraught. the dreadful Dragon, doom-harbinger, which fifteen years agone had heralded the fall of foul vortigern & his Towr, has returned & is mingled in the Cloud of towr-smoke that still blankets away the sun. its southern ally, Armorica (elsewise Benoic dubbed) is assailed by the Frænks & Ængals, & courts amity with the Gauls; meanwhile throughout its wilderness, mysterious magi have been found haunting secluded waters, known as ladies-of-lakes, and some speak of a preimmanent ***Lady of the Lake*** *beneath Ys, her face strangely recalling that of dead* ***Vivienne****. to the west, the Gæls are friendly, but offer little succour to Albions woes. to the north, Gorre churns with constant re-formation, its excess energies sapped by disputes & skirmishes with the Pictes & Ængalo-Sæxans. the latter remain split by internal power struggles, but the growing monotheistic cult of Yaldabaoth, with its worship of sameness & assimilation, begins to unite them. Albion itself, too, is threatened by power struggles as* ***Arthur*** *&* ***Anna*** *have not been seen in fifteen years and* ***Eldol's*** *regency totters. disease and draught famish the land, robber-Barons have seized control of the remote places, the people's desires are no longer coordinated, and many believe that Avalon is severing forever its tether to the World-that-Is, Albion dissolving. many of the mirror-touched – prophets, madpeople, poets, utopians, villains, refugees, rebels, mystics – take refuge in the depths of the Forest Perilous, that wood of depthless dreamlife: living either as hermits in grottos or bunkers strewn throughout it, or as wandering, errant venturers living by wondrous, objective chance. with the appearance of the Dragon, Eldol and the hierophant* ***Dubryc*** *announce a great festival where any may attempt again to draw the S'word from the S'tone – for whoever can do so shall become Arthur pen-Dragon, and lead Albion's re-generation.*

Testament of the hermit Ninnius

Discovered in a sealed cave in the Forest Perilous

ô **W**ôe pour thee reader

–,whôe'er ye be

survivor ye of Albions oblisteration

(i know not ,how in,deed

live ye't

pour th'auguries inscystant say say

likeunto veins un-damm'd we're bleeding out our days all

of darkling;,, howbeit,:
h'ere rattling my rapturdeath
,p'our thee i pen for you
th'account of Albions endays *(as*
these are certely),eht t,errors et trevaeils
our vales tormeant. &but markme: whôso in shadow
our misery guides – ? pour eft askythWort
th-Dragon *(ne'er*
since spied than vortigerns deathslide)'s stretch gums
up the firmament; frume-pen'Dragon
n,ever de'parts
,ever looms; aye it fumes *(so*
ti'said ,& weaves sssundry subtle
poysons – shadow pitchd cre*pus*cular
crost allAllbion; llofty embers its eyen
,evenowatching,
faint searing my nape ;howbeit,– harbinger
the Dragon is of ,Doom.

so'tis hence , **Y** see

,to these woodes ici haight Perilous) I hied,
likeunto other h,ermits many hundrethes *(hie*
we betimes deersome long the trails
& tydings trade ,& tales ,& heave our recluse sighs in common
downbhunkerd here ,'mong mong hisspering rushes *(hush*
*ye – even here, there's ears among the leaves)*hid
away from Albions gone vipers den, no
brython thane nor matre trust. nor nor
ne compass point
but's brushed by portents:

=> to Albions **Southly** Benoic*(but*

*each re'ports re'fusedgainst|n,other butts)*by

*(in regence)*Riothamus guided*(...howbeit by*

certainsaid by Eldol *–their consort– 'swayd for*

Albions stake– assail'd by Frænks*(in*

covert league a,vec the Sæx may be?)&

Ængals*(Sæxmates ever,aye)*&& nae thru veil of

war-lies knows how fare those fights; & eke then there's

st'ripling*(scions of both)*Budicca ,& twinnd(is't

not dodgyish...?)her brother, *Cador* lack

their dozen each s'unturns ,yet untested ;yet

most now tested the tryal rue...; :now

whoso is't in shadow our misery guides – ? *eh?*plus

,know ye newspeaks allways false ,&yet

'said tis all Armorica is is crost

of late w/crypt'ic *Ladies* sp'rung of lonely *Lakes* remote be-

guil ing gl'amour, astream avec enchauntment

e,luscive as eddies

inconfluency s'welling

w/witchery*(kindish or*

*cruelish?)*the wilds watering; & then

tis*(but where'at these Ladies ,aye...? whereby*

they rise alongside's Dragon ,aye...?

nor more ought I imply... tis eke said

these Ladies tied eache à

une Ladyofladies bound o their will;

tis eke said => cette Lady *il'l*umined ensconced

is in Ys' caverndeeps in in

th'cave-lakes deep; tis eke said*(tho*

some say the sayers ,for sæxan pay ,know

th'Americans fection her for, devise

in thus to gain their sway – or else else Gæls or e'en eht Dænes aye=> cette

Lady under-Ys in lineament

pon passedmournèd vivienne pproaches;

tis eke spoke => *anna* ,uthers

dohter 'seen oft at'r flank; but this

tis errant hogslop*(so say I)*as*(tho*

*all deny it)*to me tis dew-clear :*anna* both w/*arthur(never neither*

in 15 cycles spotted)dead*(aye)*

@*Eldols* hand be

,'r some fell crony,*(if in*

deed e'er they were at all – forfor certain

doubts by certain hermits sown

in sin'uate im'p*ostured fables ,&*

ygraines womb of dragons void

& arthur *&* anna *mere prophegandasy –*

thus wrathly now returns eht Dragon! &

whoso in shadow our misery guides…– ? so

likeliar *his* th'reads these tailes tug;, howbeit, tis eke

spoke ,in selfsame Yssic grotto grovels

=> *Merlin(rumourd* mayhap

roaming mayhap *slumberd* mayhap *slain* mayhap

*Cave-imprison'd Crystal)*on occasion ;&

who plays @ cunning out the games o Merlin? in

scrutible illuminatus!; && up

above itwists eht Dragons tailsnake;

=> to Albions ***West,wise*** Caernwellen*(vict*

im uthers *former of rapine, sorely surely nests dissent)* on tenters g'rasping

h*h*hook of regency yet hangs – wee

Mark yet ,youngling*(& tis*

'ported fulldullardly)'s by *Brastias* fosterd -~~king~~inwaitnyg*(& were* I *querried*
-mark my words twould would say
still revenge-slaver'd on uthers brood ,& all brythons else
for violence wrought on wrong'd ygraine & aussi gorlois dreamslain–also
grim sly *Ause*
childe sloughed w,w,aweful wisdoom
canniless imp halfwild madskirtynge*(many*
a-plot ,I wist,, 'll unravel Ause *anon &*
hatch'r egg of poysonplots; – plus ,mark:
whoso is't in shadow our misery guides – eh? h*h*howbeit,–
o'er the Realsea ,sowesterly th,ey say, those Gauls
w/agèd *Brynnus* at tête
ever slider close à Benoic
sea king a l ance*(but*
gainst Ængalsæx or Albion...? ; but'but
doubtless death
his hope embeds en doubts ,cause
his bed of death yawns
anon: && his scion *Bors*
champs no doubt bit, &
howso w/Benoic'll treate–?... howbeit,, norwester lie => Gæls
reneunited, rethrived ,aye
& benign ,sure – mm,yet
offstand, p'lay b*l*ind
to aught their shore licks not;
Fidelme th'bardique'en & *Gilloman* -king
cons,train t'heir scionchilde, *Gurmon*, lowlie;; so ye see:
oer Gaulande th'utmost tip
of dragon-pinion dips;, the
wingarch oer the Realsea Cærnwellen dark-pitches, beating oer Gæland.

=> to Albions ***N*orthly** Gorre*(if*

tis surely: con-fusion'd anarculture'stew

*w/fangled transdictions new)*defindsitselven never;

w/Albion in amity aye,yet

shades => brython –wh'ere's eht border lie eh? & why

on *Uriens* ,erst-pict,e rely eh...? &

why on *Rovæna* e,rst-sæxan, count eh?*(so*

say I)& whoso in in shadows our misery guides... eh – ? howbeit=> m*m*ull

on m*m*onstrous *Lot*

,t'heir hybred prodigeny, half-

thane, half-meat-childe: broody say they, choler-strung phlematic

their father favouring ,flimbsy-flesh'd ,shimmerapt, as t'were *(one hermit*

quothat choleric youth his whetblade lappd

thiseason last w/ængalosæxan bloodspurts on the borders likeunto –note

mere *likeunto*) an autre uther – tis euen

c'la/med some hermits by

,this striplyng splice of primacy

tis trulie *arthur*(*but*

tis notso quoth-I; no

pen-Dragon'sp,wrung from sæxblood!);howbeit

the Pict-March Wall dis*dis*mantled

Pictic incursionsœlicit

(*to whoso's covert benefit...-?...*)

Gorre disseminates dissolvant :here

that Dragons

head hovers's jaw snaps

his flâmecough ashes all to Gore;

=> to Albions ***Eastly*** ,the Sæxan Shoure *(tho*

*tru nruly e'en to 'emselven)*arcs long Realsea

roilsome ,volatilled ,

pinned in tegrity of knives:

Cerdic aye titled ængalosæxan *chiefofchiefs* yet

venal jackal bounds that br,otherhood'n

able *Wihtgar* æ,ngaLord therefore vies *(&*

Wihtgar *,mind, hørsas hench, practiced*

*is @ puppeting a polis eh(*plus

eht sæxan chieftain ,*Baldulf-Wispbeards* weakish simp ery*(&*

why retaind ,eh? Cerdics *mask say I;* his law

now laxifies=> sæxblood sp'ills

withincursion Albions b,orders buckle (so

whoso is't in shadow their militancy guides – ...?) now now

ccome we à *Colgrimliche*

,:sæxan avatar to Albion come

Yaldabaoth from:

eht *God* of *One*

eht *God* of *Onely*

eht *God* of *Same*

thirsty pour *veinage*

ravening pour *empyre* ;

Yaldabaoth'Un-*arthur*

crown upon *crowns:*

:*blades* upon *blades:*

:*whips* upon *whips:*

:for *closure* our *commouns:*

yy *Yaldabaoth* ,deity stillborn of th'Horse-Tooth, charnel champing

cont*agionly* cult among demoral'd Sæx rears rampant

& aye mong mong Ængals aussi

& aye mong hermits be it known*(&nothat*

I *this* Yaldabaoth *a-scribe not&yet... tis not*

the Dragon single dreadish likewise?... yet... so some

claim unstung those ÆngaloSæxans; but

mark my wordes:thereby flies
Albions doom ,vast maggot-*ch'*urn &
vat of *Yaldabaoth's* minions –howbeit,
Dragon*(Yaldabaothornot, e'en if pen-Dragon true)*s'other-wing'
s'acurled along eht Sæxan Shoure;

=> en Albions **Selfcentre***(albeit
burgeons centrelesswisse)*Dis-
solution feasts our fiber on on ,Albions
prey to t,rustbleach*(& e'en
afore the Dragon's misted withe Cloud –ne
speak o' that oft ,eh? &* whoso is't in shadow
our misery guides... – ? howbeit, ken:=>
Merlin thys decades ever been missed
aft that triad of guiDance years pour *Eldols*
infant regent ,aft that dyad o' furtive;*(–for
many & tang'led the tangles his traveils ,if
half the hermits halftruths hiss)*vanishd*(;tho
asaid, ssumed dead or crystaltrapt ,*I *ween
him* him *yanking statestrings wondrous puppet-liege
unseen – :just see* ;be,set by r'aiding ÆngaloSæx vec
barns in blaze(& even Dænes)&
harpoond fishboats scarlettering tydes ,& punditers
of Yaldabaoth the Onetruegod one by
one controverting brythons
& yet all breathe the Cloud &
ne'er eft hængist venomd Albions em'pathetic t'rust*(t'
ruth in the garrotte)*;& *Eldol Eldol* aye's regency stands yet
raggeds*tilt*ed threadborne phthisick
,*Eldol* staunchd by half too just for rule*(or
else'f* me *you'd query clever too by half,r
else'n armoured tongue f'r* Merlin *mere)*commands
but tepid staunchitude & rare rare's

a thane'r matre ne in trigue gainst him *(howbeit*
knows it he or nay) so each
phalanx floats on s'chism g'hosts w/
viesome goals jam up &
rot in spoi*led* Harmony – so *whoso is it who*
in shadow our misery guides eh – ? I name not , mark
you ,tis Yaldabaoth   Diseases Demiurge; & yet
plague cloud clogs in visduous lungflog *somehow* &
streets w/brythic corses paved, & in
the Dragons shade parchd plants
& e'en th'pests for waterdearth wither;
& then afar yond *Eldol's* way *(an autre*
ængalspawn ,these) rapine of robber-Barons ,infiltrant
of peaks & caverns ,deltas ,*b*ridges ,marshes ,wastes ,their
venture: commons de'spoilage , thieves de re'sourc age ,who
mill wo'men => machines of f'acts or facture – in
Albion by dis'cords bound turmoil-to ,atomated ,automated
Albion's this corpse we live on
Avalon abandons us
ô who scans this bathe my pity pour you
in f~~uture~~time stranded
have naught autre!

Hencely I hied me
here t'this hill w/in the
deeps & verilie this Forest seethes
w/Conquering Real's re*fug*ees :un-plumbed un-mapp'd, un-
b,bounded f,auve un-,compassed,:dub'd
Forest Perilous: abode o hermits *(misanthrop&no, some mindepriv'd, I avow,*
mystics, madwomen, martyrs, bandits,
chaunters, rebels, fantomes, erranters –
eht kindly, eht wolvish, eht grimlich, eht faï, eht
de'lightsome et daungerouse aye:

waondrous region   flowring magic
:Albions inner margin
Forest o*fo*f our Utmost Dream
ourganic canopy indwelt
w/dearest emanations daily ,by
nacht by darksome mares;
Forest of Perilous Paths – this p, lace
in dreamspace stretchd its fabric ,shifts & t'wistful torts ,so
ne'er   where you ha'e been   is there
,you once ab*sent*ed – no trail
leads twice spot selfsame thereunto ,so
venturers ever be stray ,so
vwventures ever errant go; & a a
Forest of Perilous M,*omen*'ts – in
dreamtime fogs ,in webtime stray in
timeless liminal p*lent*y
,lost ever to linear ;yet
here ne ængalsæx my thatch shall match-to, nor
no baron share my gath'red berries*(blasted though the squirel be-theive'm)*ne
be scourgd by vaast Dragorgons wrath til
all of Albion else be b'urn,d away
& bloody merely Brythain be
,pestilential body poli-tick –for via
here'screen o leaves   *alone* I
by by the Dragon
can't be seen.

howbeit e'en our **L**eaders*(if*
*leaders be en deed ,nor led by shadoweye)*see
t'horizon a boil with Albion –seize
pon the pen-Dragon'seal –as read
skywise Dragon scar,let
sound throughout th'isle: tis*(so*
pro-claim they ,but ever newspeaks false ,tis
th'augury d'*arthur(but note; –how* Dragons *but*

*D agons mask...take note,eh–;)n'*so ,now,
late@last *Eldol* regent &
Dubryc hierophant call, forepon Mayday next
un festive council @the Stoneye-Henge, whereat
eft whoso wist the tryal may
that stub*born* S'word of ste*ward*ship from S'tone
& Anveil st'rive to *d*raw, & thus-be *arthur*; or
t'elsewisse parlay *(dance ,I say,*
t'heir masters' danses);nay, no
salve's for finding thus; alls to die anon; I ,here
my lasting-days shall bide thiselfsame cave within: @hands
my bushelweave of nuts my, trove o'
berries dried m,y deerjerkstrip now shut &
trickling brooks of water creep; 'n here
await the endays pl,*acid* lie ,as
Albion rattles gorge'ous death. &
whoso is't in shadow our misery guides?... y*y*you ,fri*end*
alone in aftermath compute – pour you
the crypt is spill'd of albion, beguiling dust of charneldream
despoild its mysteries: to
autopseye di'splayed.

so scribed by Ninnius cette day
for g'hosts whate'er may survive th'impendant flâmes.

Interlude:

Anthem of th' br Otherhood of Gore

Gorish Chaunt pro-claiming Lot the vessel for Arthur imminænt

~~~~~~~~~~~~~~~~

"eded, the King succeeded!
'The Sorcerer and Sovereignty!
'Who has seen the goat bite the dog?
'O Nare Magan Kònatè!
'Will you not arise?'
Son-Jara transf"

–*Son-Jara*, as recounted
by Jeli Fa-Digi Sisòkò.

~~~~~~~~~~~~~~~~

<u>Chaunters Firstlie cHorus</u> ***<u>cHaunters Secondlie Chorus</u>***

oï: Whod'ye figur fated be"
for arthur's fΘrm to fillup?" ≈>

"næ must be arthur ≠ uther-progenie innit
<≈ *"næ legup may be's ≠ næ garegauntee innit!*

≈≈≈>So wencèlie will 'e nextlie hail?"
twillit-be aye an *ængalosæx*,sea-son axswung?" ≈>

"næ sure, sæ brast big' 't–bullies
<≈ *"ne'er beaut bedeck'll Albion innit!*

twillit-be aye>≈commin= of *westcærn* kin,"
craftful flintyfolk, cliffcoast cragclung?" ≈>

"næ limpled cærnwellen e'er'llead
<≈ *"countrie cockl'd-hornèd, cowèd innit!*

twillit-be aye scions of far-arm'd armorica"
unfixied waveticklers, post-oⱢt-embatterd?" ≈>

"næ, so seasevered shall benoic e'er see aye
<≈ *"w<eye<Albion for dint o' speck o' world-grit innit!*

sæ then, twillit-be aye th' brood of brythie-thanies,"
some figmented faïre dreamie-thwrong-mask-ghoulie?" ≈>

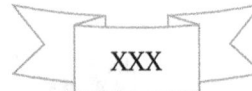

" næ, e'en pen-Dragson arthur's ren volution
<≈ *": mère ghostie; formier our wonts millennic innit!*

cHorus, cHauted in Jointlie: "I peeper'd me=> me **L***ot*"

"& arthur there divvied me, an' sought≈>"
"than ængalosæx more daughtyfought"
"than th'cærnish cronier, aye i sought"
"than armorican more morphouswrought"
"than pen'dragon purer, aye i sought"
"an arthur ripe to fix in Gore:"
"our *Lot*!"

soï: **W**h*ere*'s th*ere*for arthur tied t'be skivied?" ≈>

<≈ ***"hie ye fastish to harmoniac Gore!***

\+ thereinflows thanichor, matreplete," ≈>

<≈ ***"hereinfuses celticulant brythiculture!***

\+ hereintersects benoic quicksalver flow~ers," ≈>

<≈ ***"thereimbues cærnish crystal Ω cour'age!***

± diefuses hide-chill'd ængalosæx vybe," ≈>

<≈ ***"diesolve'em all Ω bloodculture homogenerous***

≈> *"!un*ited *in* Tin*cture of* G*ore or br'Otherhood!"* <≈

Chorus, Chauted in JointLie: *"Then blessed me aye mineselven's=>***L**ot"

": manifestfold arthur's thought≈>"
"ye than ængalosæx more daughtyfought"
"more than cærnish constancy bought"
"ye than armorican more morphouswrought"
"sundrie pen'dragon purer, tis naught"
"an arthur ripe to fix in Gore:"
"*our* Lot!"

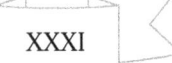

aye brustily strugglory' **D** *Uriens* an' *Vivienne*!," ≈>

<≈ "ayet mired at anarchyclepteccentricity innit;–

aye bonnie'n'b'loved they first brythonbl**ended!," ≈>**

<≈ "ayet næ let youngin-gorelings tug Albion's br'idle!

+ if elderGorre næ like it?" ≈>

<≈ "youngrim Gore's united!

+ if self-slaves harsh our chorus?" ≈>

<≈ "mut'ant forms'll melt before us!

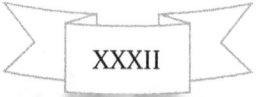

cHorus, cHauted in jointLie: "Then smooth'd√=>Perfection, ***L****ot*"

"; as arthur Gore imbodies's thought≈>"
"by lionstrikes our foes's befought"
"wit cunnin-craft our willbe bought"
"diff~used trans,parent peacelie wrought"
"i,d/eal duce death nigh,t to naught"
"They's arthur's br Otherhood of Gore:"
"our *Lot*!"

aye:-ℓwhoth'n's arthur,-**K**ing on th'thresh?" ≈>

<≈ "*tis* Lot *dis-solves essencesina*d*tomatter innit!*

aye:-ℓwhoth'n's Our thirst-killer, mindmould in flesh?" ≈>

<≈ "*tis* Lot *bullies space to commode their y'earn innit!*

aye:-ℓwhoth'n's our malgamar, who dischord tamed?" ≈>

<≈ "*tis* Lot *effaces tangles diff'errant an' s*m*oothes ch,ill peace innit!*

aye:-ℓwhoth'n'Statelie flawless lawful softlie sifts us?" ≈>

<≈ "*tis* Lot *like pl'acid water sponge absorbs con'forms us comfy innit!*

<≈ aye: arthur cr'own our *Lot*, our State :innit! ≈>

Chorus, Chauted in Jointlie: "com’posed allfrom, allform’d comes **L***ot*”

"*Arthur assimilant acts as ye ought≈>*”
"*of æng’losæx more hardie-fought*”
"*of cærnish feal more dearlie bought*”
"*of armorican moltenry purer wrought*”
"*the brythic madness trapt an’ caught*”
"*trained by th’br’Otherhood of Gore:*”
"*in* Lot*!*”

sæ then: *Lot* = arthur, an’Albion S meltsoon?” ≈>

<≈ "*aye sithen sh’all soon say th’s’Word from s’Tone!*
sæ then *Lot* be foredestin’d, an’arthur yclept he?” ≈>
<≈ "*aye soothly he’ll hilt-grip an’ tug for’that Gore-blade!*
an’ whatif the s’Wordtongue stick lies in it’s,s’Tonelip?” ≈>
<≈ "*like lock broke pon anvil we batter that bladeout!*
an’ whatif enchauntment the s’Wordins’Tone fix?” ≈>
<≈ "*pumping bellow’s breathf’ire we’ll cleanburning smiths!*
an’ whatif mystichaosubjectivation clinamen rob our *Lot* of arthur?”≈>
<≈ "*like torted snagiron flamelt t’~~SÂME~~ th’divurgent foes of th’common* **Lot***!*
<≈ "an’ Albion beat anew” ≈>
<≈ "purest steel processed thereunto!” ≈>

Chorus, Chauted in Jointlie: "oï, emborg th’advent of peacehived *Lot*”

"who’s not call’d *Lot* :‘arthur’: firm be ‘em taught≈>”
"wh’oppose ‘arthurs’ will, be ferventhey fought”
"for *Lot* let libations an’incensce be brought”
"of *Lot* let busts icons’n medals be wrought”
"let not arthur’s force flee, by Form be uncaught”
"for arthur’ll reifie th’br’Otherhood of Gore:”
"in Lot!”

II

~~~~~~~~~~~~~~~~~~~~~~~~~~~~~~~~~~~

"ravelers will form great caravans of knight-errantry in search of adventures, each displa ying one particular character. One day there may be the *Rose Bands,* who come from Persia and have a d ramatic and lyrical character, a few days later the *L ilac Bands* arrive from Japan and reveal a *poetic and literary* character; and over the cour"

–Fourier, *The Theory of the Four Movements.*

"The fool who persists in his folly will become wise."

–Blake, *The Marriage of Heaven and Hell.*

~~~~~~~~~~~~~~~~~~~~~~~~~~~~~~~~~~~

folk flock from all Albion to the tourney at the s'Tone Henge. **Dubryc**, *pre-eminent hierophant of Albion, blesses the proceedings,* **Taliesins Head** *sings from atop his pole, & the citizenry dance. the following day is given to contests in all the skills and arts of life, after which all who wish may attempt to draw the s'Word from the s'Tone & Anveil, to be designated thus pen-Dragon. as the games proceed, one obscure gastromancer,* **Caï**, *loses his breadknife, and his foolish young br'other* **Wortimer** *is sent to find it. to his dismay it is missing, and he is dismayed til he recalls, not knowing its purpose, the s'Word and s'Tone standing within the Giants' Henge.*

calloo !& callay !=> **P**rocessions wende
thru Albion bound for eht Stoneye-Henge
to moot & fest dance w*ran*gle footrace
vie jest mourn fence struggle vault
: matres , brythons , thanes , un~~sæx~~ ,
un~~ægals~~ , baron bandits – small
cenacles affinitized &
parents w/t'heir satellites &
thoughtfolk cast by mnemnomancers &
fleur-wains drawven by nurturemancers &
que'ens & -kings w/ motleye troupes &
massy phalanxes intire mount
flots & scudderclouds of tentage
sailing hillcrests & vailes ouer ,

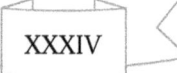

aflow below eht cumulous sky wyrm looms

t'highways teem w/peoplage : all
pack foot paths , roush eht rodewayes
clotted in amity , arms length'd be-rival'd;
some pour earnest civilicitude ,for Albion they *come*;
some for vaast dejected in dorsid shambol misère ,they *come*;
some pour carnivallic venturesome ,funfamished aye they *come*;
some for power weening ouer ,gr*asp*ish premacy they *come*;

Albion en tired throbs
à t'heart of s'Tone
see'king anna see'king
arthur
over all.

lô=> winnowing from **W**esterly
be-comes eht cærnish company:
beorny *Brastias* their head,
fond bard et re gent, theorbo-kissing
his fingers tipping, strum'd & sung'd
eht roadstreams flhush*hhhh* – & flank'd by doub'led
1.) adolesscent *Mark* on ,-kingshlip's
cusp his ,babbling ill on baubles
s,pent his tongue their f'lapping s,ail;
2.) hisistren *Ause* adolucent,
pois on verge in magick steeped
in left-wise hand, & wistely husht;
cou'sins both (thru uthers sin)
à *arthur* & *anna* 's elucive kin
,in thricewise fine afîre t'heir blood
=> rejoin that blood or lose't again.

& lô=> fro' **N**ortherly draws nearly

from Gorre a numbrous gag,gle hence:
imposing *Uriens*,   solderer of Gore,
bristlestout beard & braintorquing bellow
,skind tattoo strewn all atext with sigil;
\+ faëbrush'd *Lot* his , progeny liminal –
brood-halfing they , preen-halfing they
– y'et prickling roudabout withal
a thanic Will determina t
within the sizzlish powerpullse
of flesh – & brist
w/flush a newly sect w/zeal
w*hiss*pered: <=*here is* arthur *!* "
:so m'urged w/*Lot* the route along
un host devoted , sect & strong
w/1 led-by *morgAnor* +1 led-by
Carados +1 led-by *Nentres*;
& mid marching aye   mightlie croon
for all who list <=*aye here is* arthur *!* "
for lô they thought in fleshform wrap "
& lô tis 1st issue of newminted Gorre "
& lô tis w/prodigy shall they "
the s'Word of Albion d,raw forth! "

& lô=> eht compass all ways **S**heddes

of robber Barons venal or viol'ntous
(each un "-king" ils style themselven)
w/grimliche mercen ,Aries troupes
& shard ex*tort*ion lab'our fruits

– each of *arthurs* name[1] enamourd,
each one's fame's'ore covetous
as augured of, each lustyng d'reams
eht s'Word of Albion to wield,
forthat thereto whomeverso
should yield – dread those names bespoke
tout bas: the *Baron Crandallmas*,
the *Baron Randegoris*, eke
th'*Duke of Caudebenett*, eke
th'*Baroness of Idres*, eke
more in myriads; mais more
for-t'erroring than all (so speak
the brythons hushwise 'si de the roads)
: tis grimlich baron of barons, haight
merelie: *the [King w/100 cNights.*

& many **A**utre thousandes hied
(pas names & tales ne re-lay'd
herewitheld within here lines)
à Henge-Stones' fen: for chance
c.f. might mention make...:~ one *Clariance*
,ambitious matre + her band
who fain th'at s'Word would try her hand...
c.f. or... *Lœdegrants* eht Cærnish thane
in hopes in fluence h'ere to gain
,+ hys daughter[2] palfried mongst hys train...
c.f. or... *Ægwissance*, un~~Sæx~~ priestess
to Yaldabaoth, + her keen adepts
their temp/les God & shaman test...
c.f. or... *Bedwyn*, stalwart matre they

1 (Author'ity)
2 *haight Guenefaire*

no s'Word grasp seeks but greets that day
may grant a N'âme to celebrate;
c.f. or... *Sanam*, 'spairing brython, woe
-besodten ,wan ,elyngaliche ,broke
pon epochs w'heel ,b'led pour hope...
c.f. or... *Balan&Balin*, hap*less*t'win
rash buoy youth rare to begin
& sure eht tourney're meant to win...
c.f. or... cette *st,ranger* ,markd ,it seems, avec some task
full furtive, straunge, shadowswathed in mask
& flits to route from route, un wynking flask
hys mantle peering from; his questage none dare ask...
c.f. or else... un middling *Ector*, effish
farmer (cærnish veterrant ,yet
a'part <=\\ //=> eht cærnishcolumn)
– chirkes ceaseless he ,admonish
for his flightsome sons : *c.f.* 1.) stout *Caï*
,so goodsome boozer,[4] broalde
& fullsome gastromancer, brash
& crasslichamliche be his crust, yet
sweet the yeast him tender swells
;& grappling s'Words he loveth not
yet dreams in culinAries' contests hot
of honours garnerd, scrimmage-crumpets served; &
c.f. 2.) *Wortimer*, peekgoosen childe of scrawn
(or *Wort* ,as *Caï*-dubbd)
scarce's a dozen cycles c'rouwnd
– Worldblind Wordlorn Wildered Fool
of otherwhere dew-eyen thr'all
to otherwhen in-cessant d*r*awn
quixotic halpless citizen

4 albeit lacking a score of sunturns.

euer distrait & inutile
beyappèd by hys hound *Cabal*
who nips hys fond behind ,withal...

so Compounded Albion

t,ravels make to happy tourney
en many membres malgamate
pon Salis' meads ,pack pasturage
to rousish flocks encamp thereon
by the constellate w/massy motley
phalasteries pitched en vaast pavilions, &
betwixt, like lightningflies, gleams dust
of ssletnuoc lonefires gleam tiny bands
of motley cnights 'vec thirst pour gâmes
or gloreye, & when sembled all
en cheergreedfear mélange beneath
eht Henge of s'Tones where sandworn *Eldol*
,long-sought *arthur* reagent to,
waits notary avec his son haight *Cador*
(mi-sullen & mi-seryows youth)=>
anon ascendes with'Inner s'Tone-Ring frâmed
in sarcens: *Dubryc* , *Hierophant* :lintels in
eht: *of Albion en amor'phous masse* :the
p'*ray*er of potential p,resideth he t'here
& *Dubryc* eht festivity in highwisse praises
& *Dubryc* eht slaysport & warplay decries
& *Dubryc* eht différence en camaraderie p'raises
& *Dubric* eht purifetishes decries

& *Dubryc* eht fidelity of *Eldol* p'raises
& *Dubryc* eht rapine of barronage de'cries

& *Dubryc* eht artifacting nurturemancy p'raises
& *Dubryc* eht privatory p*robb*pe*r*ty de'cries

&=> à fin puis *Dubryc* à *geste*ur'd **s'Tone**
upon **an'Veil** insunk-to by a **s'Word**

& spake he thus: "**L**est anthee be

in somewise ignorant in this,
tis wise ,i wist, that well thee list
how comes to us cette wondermeant you see:

"euersince pen- Dragon uthers death

stands eht real*m* en jeopardy
long whiles great, et many ween
to h'ere be p*rove*d or *war*de d -king.
then hence *Merlin* hied to me
& counsels calling all ye thanes
& matres of ye realm who would,
that hie they shulde the Stone Henge-at
by Maï-Days light, ou elsewise incurl
fates pain of cursing; & for cette cause:
to s'play some miracle who might
be proved pon trials mettle right
,wise -king of Albion. so i,
by *Merlins* council, cast for all
eht thanes et matres of the realm
who would, to join us h'ere. & when
the Dance was done behold; vaast *s'Tone*
of foursquare likeunto a s'tone
of marble; and in midst whereof
was like a steel'd *Anvell* a foot
on high, et therein stuck a fair
s'Word naked by the point, & letters

s.f. setten , there=> veteran *Ector*, eyes brimburst
of *sent*iment, earen strainbended
round *Dubrycs* address
to hys civic breast-pressd;
utt*he*rapt til eht sermons well ended;
& his offsprung young *Caï* @each couplet
toasts tipple à bon pater *Dubryc*
his flasklip agape
for each linebreak un grape
& belches his loy,all huzzahs.
& eh ... rapt in reverie , *Wortimer*,
whelmed o'er the multitudes round him
si wildely wrangled
; his fancy be-t'angled
h'ears dis-course of *Dubrycs* report ne-more;
i-twix eht boys leggins like maï-poles

there were writ in gold about
the s'Word in Ysyssssssy'c ~~tongue~~ ,saithus:
S'VVV +S'SRRRF SSS–SVYT TTTFFF SSS CCCC
YTRRRTTTO+ F>HHH S'+SKRRRY , *S'P'/RRR* KS OLVYOJ TRRR .
(which is as much as cette
: '*Whomseuer this'Word should draw*
this stone herefrom eht king as should-be
shall become, from Albion
omnant collect
yaps Cabal: AARcH!AARcH!AARcH! AARcH! AARcH!AARcH!AARcH!
his mut morris-praunce be twixt em
t herefore: to-day, to-dance
et weavès hys leash
til offspringgès ye beaste
& s,tumbles'light *Wortimer* licks im,
et on gr'ass planted, *Wortimer* (*Wort*
as hys br'other hym dubb'd (for tis shorter))
spied a snail & wondyrs
could shell its be sunderd?
hys thesis exp'lored in c ourt order
yaps Cabal: AARcH! AARcH!AARcH! AARcH!AARcH!AARcH!AARcH!

wyth blunting bends grass blades he grabs at,
& dustgrit but shrinkles its skinsack
;yet hys questingmind wandres
– *Wort* winsome y-pondres
what wraiths th'eire old dusts here still clasp at

so besets him en analyse dirt
whilst o'er him a dozen folk tumbling
à middlingish hurt
then upstruck spigidehout pon the **W**inds
he remarks not the curt
aloft offsifts the *Head of Taliesin*
exc"*Wort!*" shouteth *Cai* "stop thy Bumbling!
his merry mus e'ic, en sheear de'light
vec plaintive zephrous of hys voice!
that blokes shutted up
al-wat ye stoneye Giaunts (braught
& fain wouldst I sup!"

from Gæland autrefois by *Merlin*)[5]

en ring daunce   alde-lyke   neathe sunne
,*ô wondrous round,*   et rung about
yon blues'tones=> be, hold eht thanes
& matres en anarch rotation tend
& yond arwound the trilithons
eht palmdenioj brythons circle harmonly!
our joyous orb'it frienzily sustrains
til solar=>lunar orbit yields
:fruit of stars /=>/ fond rêvealers
likeunto va,pour *dis*
-sipate en *dis*"
-order combined
;& muchel of minstrelsy pon Salis' fields
,under ,the moon.

@mÔrn=> oer Salis' fields   un-wound

thriescore paddocks pon,   th'am'*biti*ous
,& the civickeen ,the bored ,the vicious
teemeet in f'locks for heterly contest
full familial , w/*pen*nants
streamyng heraldrie en bizarrie,
en eachewisse livecraft (lativ
or frivol) urgeon't, oncheerd
by shoals of brythons thanes & matres
joyou*sang*uine manic ,f'lated,
by t'*Head of Taliesin* serenadead
(pon its pole ensconced ahigh) &

5 see thee the chronicle fyrst, 2cond volume.

proannounce each tourney wondrously
at tandem clearion *dis*tinct
:see ,***here***<= twixt hasteconstructed lists
of poplar jousters s'wiftish tilt
à hullballoo c,rowdy throngsides;
– setten ,***there*** **=>**pavilions vowed
p'our poesy, boldl*un*g'd avec be*win*ded
throats – ;see ,***here*<=** @ grove outhewn
in carpen,try to come compete –
;setten ,***there*** **=>**eht gâme of toys
by adament chortlyng toddler juries –
;see , ***here*<=** alranged & readied
be *Caï's* gastromic armory
(by *Wort* outlayed):
aye: spits pan*skill*ets spounests spatulæ
& pestlemortars sporks + rollers
saucers herbs + sugar too
,for breme the baking combatude
to come in aft o'noon:
tight-packd w/pots pon *Worts* bowed back,
low tugs *Worts* belt hung heft w/spice;
,en right hand knives
,en fork hand left
+ flour + meal beshoulderd in sacks
+ even *Cabal, Worts* bruiting hound
w/vinger-casket burthend down.
alors acrost eht meadows wend
w/swiggy gob o'thirstful *Caï*
*w*ho giggles to his skies content
& *Wort*, beburthend
drinks the Day
whose morning gob,let b'rims,

yaps Cabal: AARCH!AARCH!AARCH! AARCH! AARCH!AARCH!AARCH!

pour many-a minute
& many-an hour & many-a tipple
needs must turn ere
Caï's f,ate-full tourney;
but th'carnivals m'any a musement within it...>

Peradventure they s'tumble à concert beat pon ,throbben
& elate avec rhyth,m w/baccheic blas,t rumbleriff ,both
f,all into dtrance
– *Wort* dr*awe*s otni mane-threads lashing
a frenzifried bashing
of air his skull flashing
& he edless as heavy *Caï's* cookery c*rash*ing
gainst *Wortimers* back,
& wareless as wrenched *Caï's* cutlery s'lashing
from *Wortimers* hands,
so tops *Caï* hys mead off with *gulp* ,& *Worts* shoulders
envines soporific ,soothes: "*hark* br other ,hold 'er,
as stoon as ye moss,
my munitions unburthen –"
Wort shuoffing *Caï's* kitchen rep'lies: "thou'rt the boss!"
puis re-dauncemelée-joining neht br'others are off =>
both gallop in fernals
both slamdance inburst;
e'en eht hound *Cabal* howls
twirls w/harmonized growls
til *Caï* topples moshurtl,e*f,'l'ooring some brython*
& dauncers en domino flop liketo flat cod
ha ,observe geezers within,=>*!*
ha , setten uprisin,=>*!*
but nouthe *some brython* so sorelie begrieved
& nouthe *some brython* so sore she upheaves

yaps Cabal: AARcH! AARcH! AARcH! AARcH! AARcH! AARcH! AARcH!

yaps Cabal: AARcH! AARcH! AARcH! AARcH! AARcH! AARcH! AARcH!

w/fists ttacks ahover
she pummels Worts big br other
Some-Brython tis mighty –
& *Caï* tis (for *fightyng*)
no glutton, fun lover –

so *Wortimer* ,feline ,*Some-Brython* grasps goode
:hys claws tug her visage : her tongue of her hood
s,wings centrifugal copterquick toes spun alo*up*ft
; – &… rellleases: – shes tossed,*!,*
: ere her fall the danceherd breake
Caï & *Wort* & yapd *Cabal* make an escape.

& anon nounces Sun drawing **N**igh *Caï's* feastournament
so strushble our pair thru thaneddies at shlep
bucking folkcurrents hurr ies
Worts thought melts un-to flurries
ouer matres round brythons those br others ils lept
&so *nearly* they missed
,yet *Caï* entres the lists
& the b rethren breathe moments content.

next (*aft* un firm draw pon his pipe) *Caï* ,adrenal,
bids his br other his armory ssemble for cookyng
=>so *Wort* unventories the ordnance for meals:

item ~~:1 b'oilpot ,greasd~~
item ~~:2 frypans ,sandgrated~~
item ~~:3 skillets ,greasd~~
item ~~:4 spatulæ~~
item ~~:5 spouns ,tightnested~~
item ~~:1 spit~~
item ~~:anautre wine (pour fun)~~
item ~~:1 palm sugar ,tight canner'd~~
item ~~:7 saucers ,nested~~
item ~~:eht casket ruddy wine~~

yaps Cabal: AARcH!AARcH!AARcH! AARcH! AARcH!AARcH!AARcH!AARcH! AARcH!AARcH!AARcH!AARcH!

item ~~:eht casket pallid wine~~

item ~~:10 palms meal ,sackd~~

item ~~:10 palms flour ,sackd aussi~~

item ~~:eht casket s'lipping wine~~

item ~~:2 pestles &~~

item ~~:2 mortars~~

item ~~:2 sporks &~~

item ~~:2 rollers~~

item ~~:an autre aure wine (ye ne'er knowest)~~

item ~~:2 spounes~~

item ~~:1 spoun rag~~

item ~~:1 fork lint~~

item ~~:asst. herbs ,eachly seal'd stout~~

item ~~:3 tineforks ,tuned pour savourye~~

item ~~:asst. spices ,eachly seal'd stout~~

item ~~:1 parinknife~~

item ~~:1 skinninknife~~

item ~~:1 carvinknife~~

item :1 b*read*knife

[pause one beat.]

quoth Wort: "!*?* but where be *my* b*read*knife" :Caï *qoth*

yaps Cabal: ***AARcH!* *AARcH!AARcH!AARcH!* *AARcH!AARcH!AARcH!* *AARcH!AARcH!***

quoth Wort*:* "?!but where be *yr* b*read*knife!?" *:qoth* Caï

" alas good my b*read*knife
" velourburnishd steel!
" thine teeth so fine filed,
" def*eat*ing each heel!"

"tis ne mastry! "*quoth Wort*," :on that dauncefield lying
twas bandon'd sansnote when we took us aflying –

mae quicker ye think
i re-turn in a bl*ink*
ere your turn to go gallantly frying!"

then **S**hot·like·a·d*art·hur*ls *Wort* oer the fens
,scuds s'tonelike oer drylake à daunce*g*'round again
[in veil of matresphere
velops hys h'ere]
& en jambe flex regains cette arena of p'leiasure
but wôe be-yond merasure!
*<u>ne</u> se*rrated treasure
reclines there; doomd b*read*knife of *Caï* ,lorn for ever –!
so **B**umbled in hypervent *Wort* runs a-seeking:
& hither he rushes,
thither he hastens,
& hither he barrels,
thither hightails it,
& hither he sprints,
thither he dashes,
& hither he zips,
thither he whips
& hither he whizzes (likeunto a wind);
thither he streaks,
& hither he charges,
thither he jogs (as does hys dog);
& hither he speeds,
thither he darts,
& hither he sweeps,
thither he bounds,
& hither he lopes,

yaps Cabal: AARCH!AARCH!AARCH! …

thither he pounds,
& hither he bolts,

——————— *& infiliates a thread of rift* ———————

,then chills th'rill hys marrow ,soudden
,dredde clutch afar b'arrows
– vaast silence in tendrils like dryflake caress hym;
for all to the games but the ghosts went: alone,
& nary a citizen stirrs pon eht s'ward
,neither æsthlete ne bard.

Yet for <u>*any*</u> firm blade pursues *Wort* hys quest
for that good br'other *Caï* prove hys cookery best;
so *hither* Wort *careens,* &
thither he races,
& hither he scurries
thither he hurries,
& hither he hurtles, (basked in worry)
for all to the games but the ghosts went: alone
thither he scuttles,
& hither he scampers,
thither he flashes,
& hither he gallops,
thither he hies (likeunto lightning)
for all to the games but the ghosts went: alone;
& hither he shoots,
thither he zooms,
& hither he trots,
thither he legs it,
finding naught but allfolks exit
for all to the games but the ghosts went.

then *Wort* with ,in **P**anic

a huge loaf of granite

(or marble it maybe,

he knows no *g* eology)

s'pies in hys mnemory {reasonless surelie};

an anveil bes*tr*addles

in mindsight upon it

irony , fiery {surelie he's addled};

! et puis=> lô, a s'Word,

! hys brain t'here be-holds it –

aye ,hys eyen *have* seen it – but wh'ere – ô, *so*'s it earlie!

but s'Words're forged pour parting,

...& parting be slicing ;

...& slicing be bread-for –

...& blades for bread dicing

...& there (for some reason)

wythinen that ciyrcle

of s'tones is a s'Tone,

! & thereon (for some reason) !

! an Anv il is sittyng, !

! & therein (for some reason) !

! a s'Word has been stuck, !

! w/the which belovèd his br'other *Caï* !

! a sandwich fine shall cut !

! which shall some gut highly praise !

so Wort, passing wearièd, hys pathway makes

as if t'were he dæmonsent

to the Standing ring of s'Tones awaits

;he is there alone alone

,for all to the games but the ghosts went.

Interlude:

The Laydie of the Lesened Lake

Armorican Ballad recounting one of the tales told regarding Adylythen Ponde, in southeastern Benoic, circulating during the stewardship of Riothamus

~~~~~~~~~~~~~~~~

" her shone so bryght,
He was afearde of that syght,
For glysteryng of that wede;
And yn hys herte he thowght ryght
That she was non erthyly wyght;
He sawe never non such yn leede.
He sayde, "What hette ye, fayr lady? "

-*Emaré*, Middle-English
translation of a Breton lay.

~~~~~~~~~~~~~~~~

long's i **Q**uestethèd one lake

mislay'd w'dreams' gone chyld,
yet blyndead's wit's myne ache:
detnuah, I haunt ye wyld's,
et neuer's Laydie more's her myld
t*rain*'s of myst adorns my tarn of -wake.

ne gl*amour*'s **G**l*ow*ed's those sh*our*es upon

in childenly d*well,*sing dayes;
n'en*chant*meant'spelled's thys *p*onde
nor *sourc*ery's thrilld's those *w*aves;
et neuer's ne faï took wing 'cept swans
nor's ami*able* haunt's of lovelyng Ladie.

fr'infant i **O**utgrew's me in-to youth

et gone my sword's-to wield
'gainstrugfell'd sæxan's ruth

– til't splintear'd **B**rast's my steel

et shrackd's myne shield; so homewyse soothe
congealed woe's et weal's my soule to heal.

en **H**oelpless hunt's one day's un noise

en woodshade struck's my earen:
ô sylvansilky's voice!
evila 'vec weirdlyng's cheer –
wyth doubte ne fear thru's cloudlyngs moist
i near'd cette mere's be-guiled so's my hearyng.

et hwayt: thys pond's my in'**F**ancy kiss't

I's hied upon's again;
et lô! con*cg*ealyng mist
fog'd forth where's *n*aught had been
:une Ladie, friendlie, adornd in bliss,
to *m*end's our wöe! a'shim*mer* dis, *coursed* then:

"
my's siblyng's, **S**ooth'e yr murkysh pain! ~

~ ne sorrow's more askance ye! ~
~ pour nour*u*ishing's coolfell's rains ~
~ shall sluice thee soon's as plants ~
~ et dews enhance ye sprytes who fain's ~
~ would's dance in vively streams of nurturemancy; ~
~ ~

~ et **T**ransmutatious, radical, ~

~ *or* mist's *or* fluid's *or* ice ~
~ ir*magic*rational's, ~
~ alone might's aye suff,ice ~
~ to pryse off lies, d'read's man'a*cles*, ~
~ with's rêvemancy's limpid – friend: aryse! ~
~ ~

~ as liquid **P**liant c'lenches-flintish ~

~ -steely when's 'tis froze, ~
~ yet's patiently, by's dint ~
~ of's'lapping, sculpts down s'tone – ~
~ so fluid's flow's mer*cure*al flits ~
~ et poëmancy rinses ,out's our woes: ~
~ ~

~ so's percolant's renjoysce **C**onverge ~

~ our albionic st*r*eams ~
~ dans teemyng's current's merge ~
~ emulse our rankill'd dreams ~
~ the Real's dams to *s*i*e*az*s*e, oerfloe's our surge ~

”
~ 'tyl frees' *we*i*l*l d rev' solution,aery teems!

wh'ere'at's our Laydie passyng's **F**aire

<u>*thys* s'word's</u> me *g*ave to bear ~~
<u>thys</u> *g*lint's of moulten's earth,
<u>thys</u> song's in w*h*is*s*t'lyng aire,
in flâme's tys rarified <u>hyr</u> birth,
<u>hyr</u> glare flects wavelysh~~sways, y'et snappyth ne'er.

I's graspd thys **V**orpyl s'word in hand:

I's grimm to st'rive ret'urnd,
I's'trove unce~more's wyth war~bands;
I's bleedysh fear's incurred ~~
et haply's learnd our libreate~to land,
et burnd away's our scars!   ...yet wist I's yearn,

and **Q**uesteth I's afresh çette lake

mislay'd w'dreams' gone chyld,
yet blyndead's wit's myne ache:
detnuah,   I haunt ye wyld's,
et neuer's Laydie more her myld
t*rain*'s of myst adorns my tarn of -wake.

III

~~~~~~~~~~~~~~~~~~~~~~~~~~~~~~~~~~~~

"a king without a sword <=> a land without a king!"
– Boorman et. al., *Excalibur.*

"hirling silence settled around Jessica. Every fiber of her body accepted the fact that something profoun d had happened to it. She felt that she was a consc ious mote, smaller than any subatomic particle, yet capable of motion and of sensing her surroundings. Like an abrupt revelation – the curtains ripped away – she realized she had become aware of a psychokin esthetic extension of herself. She was the mote, yet not the mot"
– Herbert, *Dune.*

~~~~~~~~~~~~~~~~~~~~~~~~~~~~~~~~~~~~

determined to secure some kind of blade to slice his brother's bread, even if only a mere s'word, ***Wort*** *enters the deserted s'Tone Henge to borrow the old glaive thrust into the anveil there. unnatural and dreadful resonances overcome him when he touches it, voiding him of selfhood, filling him with aweful power; yet three times he attempts to pull it forth. long past the point of reasonable desperation, suddenly the s'Word gives way and slides from its Anveil, hovering free from his hand; he tumbles to the ground in a swoon.*

Tarn of g*h*rass ,the s'Tone-Henge be
 & aye a *pris*on*m* eke –
–dolmen-bars b'leak rockhewn hedges
 shadows-black cast, bleake
black reifections pon eht surf
 of grass-pond swhirl'd beneathe
& turn to c'agewalls s'tones & turf
 for all to the games but the ghosts went

so *Worts* **E**nclo'sure locks complete –

gingerrish he paws his way –
gentlie sallies toward eht hub –
tips his toes tis hounded prey –

breathes hys baite by swihush'd clum

*s*d*tumb*swal*lowing* infiliant ch'ill'dismay

for all to the games but the ghosts went

y'et *Wort* ,fool, persists

for love h*ys* br'other *Caï*

;hwæt – *th'air atoms*

sq'uirm wormush

sw eatmoist pon

Worts clamm*ys*kin

tinglish w/*p*le*ain*sure

y'et *Wort* ,fool, persists

;hwæt – likeunto

soup of eel*ectric*

slitherjolt swims

Wort thru mi sts

unsoughtforward

y'et *Wort* ,fool, persists

;hwæt – *Wort* pocketed

midst *ghastlering*

pulse pounding

of eht World gniriapsed

all fathom, pummels

Wort pulvereyes clampd

,pow er deself'd,

y'et *Wort* ,fool, persists

for love h*ys* br'other *Caï,*

pulls hym ~~s~~elf on

perfect*lie* dumb

-struck-up-swept

enravined he cringes

& euen Cabal sulks whining silence

& crawls catapillar'd &

h*ys* fleshe crawls avec eyen

lyke mothwings ghost g/azes

– *callour faï-b,utterfleye-lashes*

hys face s'oft caressant

– *col mirrorfolk-stares*

hys form ~~fingers~~-t,racing

– *ch,ill wraith-whisp'ring cryptbreath*

hys skin oiling o'er

avec their glare

– & nor 'twas nay the distaunt

silent eyen of the *Head*

of Taliesin ,highung

sentry ,static ,dumb

;ne autre thinges ,but

: wraithanes , mirrordæmons , sprîtes

folken from th'*un*worlds : –

y'et *Wort* ,fool, persists

for love h*ys* br'Other *Caï*

& hwæt w/in*verted* hymselven

in*vo*a*id*ed *Wort* b,urns

,hys fyber ashd, f,eels

h*ys* Wortself bit w/

acid vein'd in melt

à cinders h*ys* selfyng

y'et *Wort* ,fool, persists

for love h*ys* br,Other Caï

& lô imp,endyng

tri–tier *pillar*

(& shad/*ow*'d *pit*)

{: st'eel-***s'Word*** agleam :}

{: iron'y-***anVeil*** ink'y :}

{: philosophist-***s'Tone*** roughewen :}
w/eche step growes
& eche pace augmentes
til eht s'Word t'heavens c'leaves
=> til eht skies fall away
til eht anV^{e}il temper *f*,ire
=> til eht world upon'tis lain
til eht s'Tone its maw yawns wider
=> til eht Henge turns fang-ringd cave
til eht Blood of *Wort* its water
dielutges in*un*dates
& st ,retching is h*ys* hand>
& upon the roughly s'Tone h*ys* foot
hys weight thereto bes*tow**es*; <hand
tis braced the iceburn anV^{e}il; sll'*lii*ps
& <≈Wob*b*les & wi*b*b*l*es≈>&
wavers<≈&≈>w*i*vers
&<≈quivers & quavers≈>&
g,rasps @cold st'eel
g,rinds stonein hys heel
& euen Cabal sulks whining silence
& ba'lance re,gains &
th'ere
to'ward
that *thgir*-blade destined
for *bre*aching eht b'read
of hys Other
, he reaches – . . . .

ɥ^~~{\≈∞_Ω/^%o~<≈Ô_ † _Ô ≈>~o%^\ Ω_∞≈/}~~^ɥ

1

Hand

pon pom

~mel

O

tugs *R*

W ten

uous *T*

,leans

,ne budge dis

~cove*ring*;

th*rust*less he b'races

to hold from hold haules dis

~places h*ys* should'errs& p*oPs,*ocket backin,,,

sweat gobs up h*ys* knuckles runs

sheetw*ys*e the blade-stretch w/

double*grasp* wresting *W*

rainswe a t anathemæ down

pon all~s'words& all-b*reads*& all-blades to slicethemteeth

grit& he *sine*whines shrillys'li*p, s*grips

thrum of capillar*ys*well pump ruby wyvern

heaving heaving MOTIONLESS earen heating

eyen blooms in claret blottage

groans *O* frothy like a wroth bear lesioned:

« s'vvv +s'srrrf sss–svYt tttfff sss »

y'et eht s'Word yet

swithily jutt&
toil~growl phlemutter: « ***cCCC*** »
h*ys* muscles twinge *lo;c* ramp
mind strain-cram d ,mewls:
« ***Ytrrrttto+ f>hhh s'+skrrrY ,*** »
h*ys* arms a zag wrench, wynded ,w*a*t*che*d
no mortal b' y but teem'd utopians
for all to the games but the ghosts went
legs lift futî le t'wing e h*ys* creakspine
mithers gralven& sgnarls: « ****s'p'/rrr* ks olvYoj trrr*** »
*pound*blood*pound*fatigue*pound*fever*pound*thought*pound*self*pounde* d
o *u*t~
hymselven~of
arthur hatches
(he notes *he* th'
blood yolk psyche globbolalia
d'a Wash 'e h'anV il&s'Tone)
h*ys* outereyen under s*ee*a*l* still,
avec six legions eyen peers eht potent *i*a *l*te avec
allAvalons rêvel'ations thrumill'd
withinundate in tumuelt
viewen of ever h*ys* ancestorseethe
other~~world~~yng s'w,arms
eht s'Word g*rasp*eth arthur
arthur g asps et
eht s'Word pulleth arthur
from s'Tone&
from Iron'y pulls
arthur lung s
(*or* withereth)
arthur Worn w*eyes*eth thynges what
neuer were what fain
would be what neuer
are what fain would come
what neuer shall be what

fain had been, ; *R* surv*eyes*
~ in fibredream a bulk of bear ~
~ rageous mæternal ~
~ her very wyvern~spawn own she ~
~ most fondly m'angles ~
~ un~ruhtrA (*foul marauder!*) ~
~ worries her maw-in& ~
~ blade mirror mithril ~
~ slice faces sun~ ~
~ lances *pricgkl*int*ing* felds ~
~ in futurelie spyes he ,sad ~
~ s*l*ight ,slices cast~frag ~
~ ,mented paths refract ~
ed other verses un ~
~ ~writ or writ in ab
~sensce ownlie ;an~ ~
xiety in scipient arcs
k'not frazzle as
g'ordian flooded
avec hurri
,canes of dew,
slide athwort cette
stamen~s'Word
gleamstem
steels talk
in Anveilsoil rootbranches
meristem mithril gr*asp*ing&
straight~*snaked* razorootap
rockthRust fast this fist~within
arthur seeder of s'Wor*l*ds
arthur feeleth un~squirm
convulsèd blade liketo viper:re'coils
whissp'ring≈> sophia ~ gutted
blaze of potence t*err*ible

eht shifts imp≈

~losive catacl*ys*m ʃʃ ~erceptivel*y* *s*lithes

s'light fricte r*asp*ly

stirrs tightly power *slither*

arthur swiftbuoy surfaces bubbling

blood roars~~hys~~arthur's brainwa*ys*

>>>ô , **neue*rmore!***

y'et s*tor*uggles *w/*s'Word

keels unhanded o'er on h*ys*

back dro ps =s'>Word=an>V^{e}il=s'>Tone

& *ort*(sh'ac hen ,ashen)sways et twitch adaze

con-/f,used s,ore addled otherthanselving

. . . til mere un echo brushes hym with *Caï*

for bread blade br other lorn

& *Wort* fool sub*lim* e

upclimbs once more

et yeorneth bitter an,other-try

but bolster-grasps th'anV il gainst

& stretches forth h*ys* hand again:

ɥ^~~{\≈∞_Ω/^%o~<≈Ô_ † _Ô ≈>~o%^\ Ω_∞≈/}~~^ɥ

2

s*core*ches *s*lice hym thru sc*rat*ch arthur whisstle rip h*ys* clamp reflex grippe phalanxes from bone h*ys* handes ~~out~~sp'read digits forth as nerve paths yearn ~~out~~ g,listen ≈> singing glaive {mirror-face blade ,fourwisse angled ,h*ys* face therein re*fra*gct*ment*s sear} st'rains sunlaunce cast en,chauntment of Giants cavort isolated throngstare *W fears* tug rag shad, ow désespairation lintels crouching g'rope hunch hauls ice fang sunk *they watch* nor will relent *mind slaying fear* he breathes *they watch* sw'eat iron panic burn *they watch* *O* fool per c*ys*ts pour âme th' ther *fear death-diminutive grants obliteralation total* arthur there tips-fingers presspad ~~uthers~~ s'Word gainsting'led ex,tends h*ys* phalan x ges hilt from *palmpommelmelded* *my fear is my face* pour arthur est his s'Word {his ~~fathren~~,s'Word}*phantomist of murmuration* careen pulse *over me and thru* me hulking fauve *in their plethoræ* power less bounding vision swim d breaths flail thick upon h*ys* nape lungf,lags coal f*ill*ed *gr,asp flick fendelous, puuullls'train muscle sear atavis tic scavengers my patres ô my matres specktres pluck my fleschunks* screech wrench feel th'anguish of barrowights stro-*king* h*ys* hide arthur*[-itna]* ekohc ch'ill *R* en*te* a rror'd heaves *i will turn my innereye to* glympses of *others* mémoires of *others* chimères percieves *three-myriad tongues of light awrithe within my mouth* in-finitude of d,reams of *s*crypted fate of *others* phantaseyes horror sp,ills of *others* phantasmagore poor w'racked shock *it will not cease* out-~~selved~~ ~~be~~-buffeted w/being-shards hurld chronophotographic cells of *others* selvyng-forth *to see its path* & *Anna* pre-pres*ci*ent of Avalon pon philosophist mortar-s'Tone w/weight'y Iron'y pestle ground's the boy whom arthur burns *wh'ere the fear has passt only* wythin the pestle s'Word draws arthur n'aescent from eht s'Tone sings forthe arthur'senses testingly *to~be* ,tis primally naught but a g'rip of will, & a laugh tis dying ,*i shall not remain* & the s'Word to hym speaketh abyssal in*ti* a *mat*e depther than th'ought fills eht vessel h*ys I* had been: ***«s'vvv +s'srrrf*** **»** en,thr'all w/eht s'Word mutters nervetrails gilding visionæry wilde fragmeants deathflash ***«sss–svYt tttfff sss»*** badon g*s*/*rip* chivalry ***«cCCC»*** daunce counsel mirror asp frith ***«Ytrrrtttto+»*** death marched constantine *un-ruhtrA subject-haunter ghoul* i host an endless host be-hold in wolde yondere futureforest fearlesstrut ô burstl*ys*h arthur–bear of brythic Albion ursa-wyrm cærnwellen born bark shuck bolde baron beorn of forest perilous pulling eht pommel at ,heart gasped with pumping ,***«f>hhh s'+skrrrY»*** , f,lush w/feverd reams whileat wheezes it eases it eases it eases in æthyr enclasped by enochian grasps cram gainst arthur budgeases it eases the eidolons beckon howl rêvenant arthur *app* r oaches & pen-*{ul*timate sq' heezes *or* ether-to gather resisacrifictitious vaporescent victim W ort rec *oil s* in anguish'arch fin,gers wrench hilt-from s'Word away drops and it falls it falls it falls in Iron 'yclasped upon s'Toneye cold slab away arthur away tumbples Wort into hymselven last ~~living~~ wisp fail fades is a cave by haollowèd waters roded rises in some ~selving≈semblence~ faint thought fragments navigates says innerlie *Caï* br'Other *Caï* & hys tourney hys crust et so shudderly rheum-wrackèd chatterling pulling h*ys* frÂme from the s'Oil Wort ,precocious bleachy lamb before the anV[e]il'd Altær-s'Tone stands alofteye g,lances grimliche ouerlooming s'Word et g,rasping apprehesitant to ward th'austeer angles d'Albions cleaver mithril tempest focal mote reaches:

ɥ^~~{\≈∞_Ω/^%o~<≈Ô_ † _Ô ≈>~o%^\ Ω_∞≈/}~~^ɥ

3

\ **!** *tz* **Z** *c*hzsssszz szszZszz~~

! voltyng his veins~thru

pool of s$_s$t^{t}ing hov'ring , hung

samite~like unseen s'Word~from,

s*warm*statics h*ys* *f in* h gers

bolts[z] *burn tendon threading*

twist*or*ting *en* agony

W *or*t is *un*woven h*ys*[s]

adtoms *re* th reading as

arthur suckles en aorta of fire

W *or* t re~fused as lost

arthur d*arc*k seed tossed

in to heaps of hopeful cinders

blown into miracules of mirrorglass

& ra rock crush dans furnace melts

& e of W i re~folded hammerd

throbb'en hys ear

skull buz$_z$^{z}z$_w$rung w/foam

& re~folded & temperd re~temperd
til / tis naught but
a trace of f'led
a die late aft-i,mage b*urn*ed
pon th'eyes of arthur, yet un-oped , & fades
& th'eyen of arther, yet un-oped
be ' hold
: ô alack ô woe ô alas :
≈>s'Word ' heavens ' wrist ' anVeil ' middlearth ' ~~body~~ ' s'Tone ' deeps ' self<≈
all all : obscene balloon
malgneficent parasite chute
gorging pauncheous tick
vaast dream of æthyr lartsa speech
un~mot'*e*
allone
imp~
*ossi'*ble
sang'able
flesh'able
un~mot'*e*
:arthur:
floodrownèd in Other
spongedrunk in others
arthur ≈ un-mot'e of Albion, mot'ive
arthur ≈ s'Word of Avalon, generatious
arthur ≈ cruci*ble*fix'd Avatar, syncrethetic
mask of endless generation,s
invisible progenies prodigies
h*ys* *Wor*n subjec*t* c'leaving
arthur
in *antidentity* e:*merges*
w/≈>shriek of feckless ~~being~~*!*, seizes
the ~~body~~ which he ~~is~~ : he is

eht   of the s'Word
& Albion finding
itself arthur
Albion is every, all,
& Albion in
fuses avec arthur is the s'Word is Albion
& Albion finding
arthur finding itself w/
un-mot'*e* of good of
Avalon wistes its generate sigh
& out from eht unflexing clutch of rock
& out from eht torturing pummel of iron
liftes the fist of Arthur & the s'Word
e lides et loftes em
à the skeyes applause
brazing   skrining   sheening*!*

& the boy
direly tran'slated
emp'tied sensef'led groundf'lops limp
numbminded , rebooted , gulping in shadow
& none but cowed *Cabal*
(faint whining oer his heap o ~~master~~, all unheeding)
to hear the *Head of Taliesin* cavort in weirding-song
& none but cowed *Cabal*
(soft nuzzling at his lump'd companion, all d*ys*tracted)
to watch the Giant-s'Tones juggle lintels spritely dance
for arthur & eht s'Word
& Albions scintillant despairate chance.

IV

~~~~~~~~~~~~~~~~~~~~~~~~~~~~~~~~~~~~

"t is no mastery,' said Arthur, and so he put it in the stone; therew

[. . .]

Kay. 'Alas,' said Arthur, 'my own dear father and br other, why kneel thee to me?'

'Nay, nay, m"

–Malory, *Le Morte d'Arthur* .

"is little enough pleasure out of living. Yes, and you and I need this little time to become acquainted be fore I recede and pour out through your memories. Already, I feel myself being tied to bits of you. Ah-h-h, you've a mind filled with interesting things. So many things I've never imag"

–Herbert, *Dune.*

~~~~~~~~~~~~~~~~~~~~~~~~~~~~~~~~~~~~

***Wort**/arthur returns to the games with the s'Word, regarding it with hatred, dread, & guilt. his mind still shambled, he comes to **Caï** & without thought hands him the s'Word. Caï, expecting his breadknife, berates him for his mistake until **Ector** recognizes it. much confusion ensues, and **Dubryc** calls all to the s'Tone Henge, where Wort and any others may try again to re-draw the s'Word. Wort does so, followed by 60 others all of whom fail. still, many hesiate to accept the unknown adolescent as a pen-Dragon, and civil war threatens if his identity is accepted. **Merlin** appears, reminding all that whomever draws the s'Word must still prove their worth before receiving Caiburn from a mysterious other, only then becoming true pen-Dragon. a new contest is called for the winter solstice; again the result is disputed, & a third contest announced at Mayday. the same is repeated, & arthur's investure is announced for Lammas time. with each draw of the s'Word, Wort's consciousness is further absorbed into that of the emeriging **Arthur**.*

so fr'ail arthur **F** orged

is, pon th'Anveil of Albion,
so born from ~~wort~~
(poor larval youth)
from brythains s'Tone scullpted;
Avalons'Word d,read arthur
desperate awriggle dans
wort yet *s,tumbles* yet *again*
eyen egg-widte ('cause arthur
spies out from in ,side'em)

but wort is but
:a cyst of innocence aburst,
:a chrysalis to first its rip,
:a sentient skin begun to shuck,
& s*huff*les
sore drownd in stun
mid felds of s'playedout naught
for all to the games but the ghosts went
& wort t,rails tailike in dusts
that s'word for cuttyng b*read* he's won
& v*ague*ment thru selfyng dull
Wort **C**urseth's'word & th'bread to cut
aye from pommel down à c'rust;
for mickel mist hys mind beclogges
w/maybe painflush throbbes
or hopefold hapwise hummingbuzz
that c'laps hys skull w/maybe
hate pour cette s'word hym blazes
as bowed beneathe lintelooming giants'tones
he presses otni shadowes
asphynxiate tenebrous of velvet lungs
w'edged twixt rock&null,
y'et *wort* ,Fool, persists
for love hys Other
gainsthru ;menhir ;pressure ,h*un*ches *f*
*re*ebroke from Henge-gr*asp* @last –
Wort cuts w/s'Word
from th'Henges thrall &
straight a,way sp*ills* inky **D**read the air in fuses lit
lyke hisses atmosfearful fl*ail*s
worts c*ring*ed innerears

terrorthrobbblade dragging nail dirtboard screeching

yet aye to else stillence awaiten

for all to the games but the ghosts went

lyke that anxietous quirming mist

broad cloud-scoop stretch'd desolate

('cept fadingthane *Wort* & *Cabal* ,oblivious canine)

from Henge-end nigh to tourney-c'rowdy-end

hunchd wort runs lyke bat-batter'd

stbumbles in tremulous cower s'Word

clutchd clumsysh to stummych

all ablubber for nâmeless-*Los*s

but up bubbles arthur in hym brave;

& wort in whimpers writhes & wastes

but thys hilt tearrible arthur g'rips

& roused in stride crost salis plain

w/wort hys body limbp'd in tow he wears

til gradely eht roarswell thousand tonguèd maw

wrabpout him, c'all of Albions tourney beast in riled quest,

hys eyen dis-Clouded-un, wort saw

again w/in-eye: matreshadows, thaneddies,

again w/out-eye: hulks of flesche-folk densely,

felt hym bumpd'n tumbld to s'oil, well spilt

& besodded w/blockheady Guilt

& arthur wythin hym re-coils

abject as styrofoam lovenote gremlin , wort lurches scamperawling

bathes hym in shamefaces'

eyen shedding tears hys cloak shreddily

for theft *for* bumble *for* dreamingday *for* diffèrence *for* tahw-ton-swok-eh

he does *for* arthur within hym.

til wort enꝤr ottled by humble

scurrying buggily s*LAP*s|

|*Caï*'s *bac*kinto

,st*un*|ned!

"*oï! wherefore* Wort's *ye diddly fuckin daddlin?* :barketh ***Caï***

{one peeper mere pon *Wort* , t'other pon festivals panoply}

– hath fetchd thee me me breadknife, br other?"

& weakneed *wort*

dumbstruck repeats: "?b*read*knife br'other

*read*knife br' "

& qpueering *Caï* quizzles finely,

spies that cloakfold's

g'lint crouch fugitive,

"*ay, there's it – heft it hither –*" : ***Caï*** half-distract

& wortstuttring: " *read* if 'other "

as hys hand hys s'Word hands o'er in in,nosense un,to eht hand o'***Caï***, ex-

-br'other everdeferent,

yet gummed in dream ~

dim lovesheen gleams

thru arthurmist, tugs

hym bhackup from un~

dertow, b'links bubbles

knows: 'aye, i be *Wort*

,for *Wortimer* short

& these, belovèd be

(now upbraidyng me).'

"*but forsoothe, ye fool!* :-claims

tis never my knife, thys toothless blade!

such cumbersome cutter ne'er was made!

ne serrate thys, nor saw thru c'rust!

I'd deign ne split a biscuit thus!"

& ***Caï*** pon *Ectors* elbow yanks,

th's'Word in *Ectors* fist he thrusts – thus

"*hark father,* Wort *hath ruined us!* :***Caï's***

see!=> no breadknife thys bulky glaive, :harangue

nor ever yourn'or mine!..."

& fleetlike , clarity [*Ector* halfeye-roving nods uh huh]
yea hys id,entity "*...look pops! tis took! what sigil's this?*" <= points ***Caï,***
tenuous, resnared; piqued w/smug;
Wort rewak'end "I nary know son, hush. I wa'aaait...–?!" ***:Ector***[*mm-hm*]
hys falther watches & lo:**D**ownfall *Ectors* eyenballs ;*Caï's* cockcrest falls
fearful quakened – roll agon-eyes'd portent-brush'd,
t in thundrous, agog, *Caï*
e flicker-storm-crossd fate crushtickling
r face rains tears sees *Ector* see
r mouth awful awrithe Wort, sees
o hoarse worming rictus aghasht scragglyng
r horror a cave bellow sigh dark
i à fin w/spasm struggle fierce dart
p form ***Ectors*** lips five syllables: th'erefrom
p « **how got ye thys s'Word** ? » . . .

Wort qu["*twas i! aye jest, ha see, ne mete out censure on'im...*" :*Caï* martyrs
{*thys scene's*}=> Wort quivers savvy
{*by one seen*}=> sees precious hys'Word'seized
{*haight* Bedwyn *gapes*}=> by envyflare, grasp'reaches...
{*calls breathsqueezed wheeze:...****Ector*** echoes passionstruck:

« how got ye thys s'Word ? »

"twas found nigh we spotted it,snakelie in grass, must some geezer've le..." :*Caï*
croak "*hwæt!*" *:****Bedwyn*** & *Ectors* ken con'firmd
"tis drawn! by art or & sudden then *Caï* ken'd it –
strength or craft thys s'Word – *Caï* ,struck
that s'Word from ,sad-sudden warthur's
s'Tone at last!" doom of truth, knew –

anon   all Salis' flock suspressens round, tense p*lea'd*emanding:

« how   got   ye   thys   s'Word   ? »

"*twas never I,I wist;*   :*Caï* fesses

but Wort*.,,iimer hence hithered it,*
nor ken I whence,
forswappening a knife I missd...................."

& boom behold! vaast basin of brythons **B**oiling etheesa!
s,urge of uptidings   roarous oracle   in congruous congrestive!
cackl*l*aughter   whoopcries   hopehowlsnarls   anathamæ!
cLot-air thick with thanic fervor
& wort all slaught agawk asway
so *Dubryc*
pierces w/
bleating pipelung th'tumult's grumb,
& all to the Henge re–call
at council th'Testyng Game to play
so all from the games to the ghost-danse went:

wh'erefore Albions **C**acophonies hiegh at t'Henge
Wort *tugg'd par weepyng* Caï+Ector *,dazed*
s,wept by airtorn conpro tempest bellows
festoon'd unheed anointed virginous
boistral bacchic epoch storm*cloud* swells – but
lô! all ready   slow the singing s'Tones
their daunce of plodding for*tune* giaunt weavesteps sedulous in ring
th'air's a vat of *th*r*umming, rock steps thump on soil humming – &
Wort *entrancled bundled at th'Anv^e il altar, s'Word-shorn*
lô! all ready craning crooning's
Taliesin's Head : Albion's bodiless bard

Taliesin's Head lauds convivi'ally arthur, laughs
th'Anv^e^il for alteryng, tempern, hammern

Taliesin's Head w/arthuraugur's joy sings down awed assembly
kneels Wort *brow bows nape baring for th's'Word*

Taliesin's Head sings:

« !! evohé eloi !! »
« !! the s'Word from the s'Tone has sung !! »

th'Albionfolk **D**rawn

round *Taliesin-Head'*drawn
in chattring's orbit throng;
thys crowd expoun'd riddle
from *Bard-Hea*d'raws giggles
& tauntograph songs;
puis upupup's pushed Wort at eht s'Tone
cflaspt by *Caï* ~~frat~~terly
puis upupup to th'Anv^e^il's passd
em*brast*ced by *Ector* ~~father~~lie
puis upupup poised pen-s'Word
(sæxslay-blade of uther mournèd)
by ***Dubryc*** driv'n,
who augrous declaims

puis: "*thou*
,boy – *'Wort-*
-imer hight: be for
Albions people
here sembled, canst
thou draw for
'th from thys
Anv^e^il's'Tone thys
s'Word of mast'ry?"

"tis no mast'ry"   :notes Wo[a]rt[hur]

& up right re ,plants

=puistabackingreetinganveilslidesmoothstablade=

>*in drawnbreath all*<

asks *Dubryc*: "*and*

canst like thou wyse

redraw forth new?"

"aye sure"   :quoth *Wo[a]rt[hur]*

& hwæt! he drew't

a gain, nor strainèd twoo;

& peal ne bells upon peal of laughterains *Taliesin's Head* à dourfacedoubt!

& th'C'loud of storm descends

oer Albion'ssembled, vie upon vie,

pon each oer each contends

& envious each enlusts to try =>

of Threescore brythons & thanes & matres & sundry autre

tempt/ed *t*heir tryall

cette wyvyrn blade pon pry

yet ne wrigglinleast aught:

ne: wort-br'other *Caï*

runnelcheek yet

grap'ples eht blade & f'ails

& Taliesins Head *laughs*   *hys headoff;*

ne: *Brastias* unsure   yet

yif *Wort* = wigglybabe

he bore so brief of eld,

g*rasp*es eht s'Word & f'ails

& Taliesins Head *chortles*   *hys headoff;*

ne: inkyskin *Uriens*

Gorre-mason glooming
g,rips eht glaive & f'ails
& Taliesins Head *titters* *hys headoff;*
ne: Baron *Caudebennett*, eht
No–Body of Bernicia,
hauls'im th'wea *U*pon & f'ails
& Taliesins Head *guffaws* *hys headoff;*
ne: *Ægwissance*, sæxprophet, seeks
her sects assent–but breaks
her rep' thys'Word pon:
drags eht brand & f'ails
& Taliesins Head *cackles* *hys headoff;*
ne: *Balin* twin–half
bumbleaming youth,
wistyng just hyr fun
tugs eht steel & f'ails
& Taliesins Head *chuckles* *hys headoff;*
ne: score'pon score heave
ere lunar arc's lower
nor that drag'on pin shifts une tittle;
anon à Wort <= addresses ***Dubryc*** :

"*thou* 'Wort-
-imer' *haight: be for*
Albions people
here sembled, canst
thou re-draw for
'th from thys
Anv^{e}il's'Tone thys
s'Word of unmastred
by else our company?"

"tis no mast'ry" :Wort *repeats*
& lô from iron th's'Word un-sheathes
& peal ne bells upon peal of laughterains *Taliesin's Head* à dourfacedoubt!

towit=> to fiersome **Q**uarrel ruptes all

& choler'd vieship:

certainfolk w/Baron *Caudebennett* spew

thys youth con*tempt*ment bilous pon

as pasty untried urchin fishfresht patsy

& surelie som*ease*lie thane'*s pawn;*

certainfolk other w/*Bedwyn* cite

the pen-s'Word-dragons oracle own,

plead selvidence reve¡aled cette miracle shown;

certainfolk else w/*morgAnor*(boon

Lot companion)some pLot p,resume

,thys glamour mere grease&pulley matter,

sleazed s,hammery spectacle only –

so seconds

shamed *Ængwissance*

(abandon'd of acolyte

,cult-shorn by s'Word-th Wort)

,assured tis chicanery

ven*iale* of varlots;

yet tyrade's bestopper'd by *Uriens* Gorre chief

who ne'll beshittin on childen on shakydirt

nor unfolknown in sult'em cept farly in quest –

tis propd by *Lot*,

Rovænna'scion (star

in many eyen shockd

they s'Word ne tried)

advysyng skept yet caution

,'minds of millions

ab'sent ne'yet tried;

certainfolk other w/*Ector+Caï*

aspersions spurndigustethed

& Wort clear straightway acclaim ap arthur –

& fin'ally *Brastias*

,arthurs flickernurse,
thus inclines –
& aye grasp frankwise
Albions bulk
thys party-to;
howbeit
brust w/mighty
yon glowerd
p$_r$etty-kings
& barons filed
counter bring
wars uncivil fiat –
so *Eldol* un-
sure flummocks
what to do...

*~ **H**ark thrummyng-to benearth now~!~*

~how g,rave s'Tones dance roundover us!~
~how lintelimbes overound us weave!~
~how gravelie th'Tones voice rumblyng!~

lô: under rock-hued mantle su*dd*enoted
all eht host by, here behold=≈≈≈≈≈≈≈> bent
thane in shadow guilt-flask g*limp*sd
@belt, beh*oo*d'd, fulgurant; steps
all ken) @du*sk*glare's tip (*afore*
unveild's) to th'*H*enge-*h*ub – lifts (*hys veil;–*
–;ne may) ba*ck*cowl-lip: bares (*but be*
un bla*nk*·m'a*sk*
of pâr*ch*ment pre*ss*d
un-featu*rèd* ab*yss*
mad magus) :tis *Myrlin* (Merlinus
re-turnd:

now strud to s'Tone-foot *Merlin* Avalonsacred tongue invokes ,blankmaskd;
now stond in anV'il-shade *Merlin* Arthurverging'host evokes ,blankmaskd;
now stretchd s'Word-gesteth *Merlin* Albi ontic camp bespoke ,blankmaskd:

now ***Merlin*** minds 'hem:
'tisn't Caliburn[6] stands enanV'iled ,ne –
,tis hid, arthur-awaityng
hys furt*h*rance to test;
thys blade's but à battle,
brand for mere barons;
thys s'Word-game pays contingent fruit
yet pro-vision,all victors t'heir *vert*ue
prove à un-fo*re*seen hour
& utterlyond hys power;
yet & yet the bellowrancor grumbs & gryndes gainst thys unken'd -king;
so *Eldol* counsel-forged w/*Merlin*'nounces
cette compromwise:
pon Solstice tyme
pour second round thys ring'll gatherall
& any who wist'll play
& *Wort* or whomsoever
will , will Will invest that day.

Four chewed moons in h'orisons maw
herald sicklishrivelled Sol
à pinpoint cloudscreen shiver grind;
en core d'Albion
drift *on*ce more thru Sols't ice snow
:eht s'T*one*s al*one* by cold unclenched
whist crowds in c'luster gambol *f*rigid warm
w/harsching voice of d*rag*onC'loud
& lofted *Head of Taliesin*
notwithstanding galebit flesheface

6 for Caliburn al'one a penDragon may de*sign*ate.

howbeit lankhair , beard , lash , neckstump   deckd
in tufts stalactitic icicle
in spitely t'ear-frost eye-glaze wide
hys peal ne bells upon peal of laughtersnow *snows* à dourfacedoubt!

thys **C**'loud of storm inblends
thru reAlbion'ssembled, vie upon vie,
pon each oer each contends
& envious each enlusts to try =>

of **F**ivescore brythons & thanes & matres & sundry autre
*re/*tempt*i*ed *t*heir tryall
cette sæxhacken blade pon pry
yet ne budger it à bit:
ne: spirial cærnthane *Lœdegrants*
'v bitious bounty liberall
*g*rap'ples eht blade & f'ails
& Taliesins Head *re-laughs   hys headoff;*
ne: *Cador* ap-*Riothamus,*
juniorer *wort* than e'en,
g*rasp*es eht s'Word & f'ails
& Taliesins Head *re-chortles   hys headoff;*
ne: scrowlering *morgAnor*
spleen spitting gorelyng
(foremost o' zea*Lots,*
rasher than'ys mentor)
g,rips eht glaive & f'ails
& Taliesins Head *re-titters   hys headoff;*
ne: Baroness *Idres,* sternumb
Alt·cult's spydry tyrant,
hauls'er th'wea*U*pon & f'ails
& Taliesins Head *re-guffaws   hys headoff;*
ne: *Sanam* ,Guinntuics refugee
whose duct tears grease

eht blade but shan't ease: she
drags eht brand & f'ails
& Taliesins Head *re-cackles hys headoff;*
ne: *Balan* twin–half
bumbleaming youth,
wistyng ne'but hys fun
tugs eht steel & f'ails
& Taliesins Head *re-chuckles hys headoff;*
ne: score'pon score heave
ere lunar arcs lower
nor that drag'on rod wobble 1 jot;
anon à Wort <=:re-addresses ***Dubryc*** :

"*thou 'Wort-*
-imer' hight: be for
Albions people
here re-sembled, canst
thou re-re-draw for
'th from thys
Anv^eil's'Tone thys
s'Word so re-mis-tried

by else our company?"

"tis yet no mast'ry" :Wort re-peats
& lô from iron th's'Word re-re-un-sheathes
& peal ne bells upon peal of laughtersnows *Taliesin's Head* à dourfacedoubt!

towit=> to fiersome **Q**uarrel reruptes all
& choler'd vieship:
certainfolk w/Baron *Crandallmas* make sist:
on prove of Power positive lean
else martial , else bureaucratechnocrat
nor games of s'Words & iron pon'd;
certainfolk other w/*Cador* declare

by twin-tryall arthur de-cided there,
& call hyswift in, vestiture;
certainfolk else w/*Nentres*
(compaminion of *Lot*)p'resume some pLot
thys hokum greasy pulleg matter
sleazed s,hammery spectacle merelie –
– yet tyrade's bestopper'd
by *Rovænna,* Gorre chief, dis*m*^{iss}*al* rageous
at im'poli$_{s}$tic^{k}ing gloomysh;
certainfolk else howbeit her scion *Lot* mutter
,meld of brython, arthur he sembles more
ever than b'lankly thys measlysh Wort;
howbeit *Lot* Gorre-heir escheweth
cette con'test, ap-foolysh's ,
yet bites their tongue on arthur ;
certainfolk other w/*Brastias*
wrankle thys rep'tuous d*e*-alliance
as Cærnwellen in arthurs denial re-betrayèd –
he rails sly churlysh delay;
& aye t'grasp frank,
Albions bulk
thys party-to;
howbeit
rebrust w/mighty
yon glowerd
p$_{r}$etty-kings
& barons refiled
counter rebring
wars uncivil fiat –
so *Eldol* re-un-
sure reflummocks
what to re-do...

whileat *Merlin* ,mounted pon **O**rate, re-minds 'hem:

tis ne Caliburn stands ici enanV*e*iled –
,tis hid, arthur-awaityng
hys excellerance-test;
thys blade's but à baron brand mere;
thys s'Word-games fruit'sweet just pour *vert*ue
& avec proofs far yond *Myrlins* power;
yet & yet the bellowrancor grumbs & gryndes gainst thys un-kid -king;
so *Eldol* counsel-re-forged w/*Merlyn*'nounces
cette com*pro*mwisse:
@ Maydays Fest next
thys ring pour third round'll re-gatherall
& any who yet wist'll re/play
& *Wort* or whomsoever
will , will Will invest that day.

1 **Q**uarter o' moons uproll balleye'd balloons
à herald vertigruent May's
Day en core of Albion
upsp*ring*reen myriads hie
:eht s'Tones' festoons imbrace the skies
whist mobs o' lustry burgeon balm'y
& lofty *Head of Taliesin*
'vec sunray kisses graced hys face
by breeaze caressedt hys beard hys tresses:
hys peal ne bells upon peal of laughterains à dourfacedoubt!

yet **C**'loud of storm *fer*ments
thru re-re-Albion'ssembled, vie upon vie,
pon each oer each contends
& envious each enlusts to try =>

of **T**enscore brythons & thanes & matres & sundry autre

re/*re/*tempt*i*ed *t*heir tryall

yet ne shiftes it slight:

ne: steamskulld thane haight *Eglam*
detournied his feud-from whim
grap'ples eht blade & f'ails

& Taliesins Head *re-re-laughs hys headoff;*

ne: *Naram*, meet glazier,
hys boistrousbuds push's to'it,
g*rasp*es eht s'Word & f'ails

& Taliesins Head *re-re-chortles hys headoff;*

ne: *sch*emetic *Crandallmas*
spyder-subtle gorelyng
(zea*Lots* aspirant)
g,rips eht glaive & f'ails

& Taliesins Head *re-re-titters hys headoff;*

ne: eht *[King w/100 cNights*
,hoarsehowlyngs round hym
,banshee-call'd baron
hauls'im th'wea*U*pon & f'ails

& Taliesins Head *re-re-guffaws hys headoff;*

ne: *Clariance* ,craftysh
plies precisioned endless techné
– eht blade w/mechan, but shan't it ease: she
drags eht brand & f'ails

& Taliesins Head *re-re-cackles hys headoff;*

ne: *Lot,* longwatch'd
their cu*ltfolk* "*Lot*" chau*nt*,
*scoff'scaffold-s'T*one mou*nts*
ye*t t*ugs eh*t st*eel & f'ai*ls*

& Taliesins Head *re-re-chuckles hys headoff aye & aye & aye;*

ne: score'pon score heave
nor glad*i*us stirs;

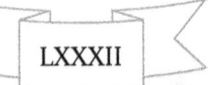

anon à wort, re-re-addresses ***Dubryc***:

"*thou 'wort-*
-imer' hight: be for
Albions people
here re-re-sembled, canst
thou re-re-re-draw for
'th from thys
Anv^e^il's'Tone thys
s'Word so re-re-mysteried

by else our company?"

"tis yet no myst'ry" :wort re-repeats
& lô from iron th's'Word re-re-re-un-sheathes & frees
& peal ne bells upon peal of laughterains *Taliesin's Head* à dourfacedoubt!

towit=> to fiersome rereruptes **Q**uarrall

& choler'd vieship:
certainfolk hie to *th'[King w/100 c'Nights:*
hys hoardes à shoreup gain,st Sæxan Shoure
& for feodage opt oer civillviolenced menace;
et certainfolk else w/*Carados*
(*Lot* crony fond)precieve foul pLots
Merlin twixt w/Brastias'r'Ector'r'*Lœdegrants'r'r'r'r'r'r'r...*
– sly shadowcrafty cardmark spectacle –
& manyfolk yet *Lot* , icon of Gore,
invest w/*faith* th's'Word lost from'em
– lost when *Lot* th's'Word lost –
spurn arthur be not arthur *Lot's*
& dheeap despise thys measlysh wort;
et *Lot* of Gore deny ne more
tho by t'heir tacit sires'sighlence
to t'heir allies turned
,for pre-sent lie;

yet *m*hostfolk w/ *Cador* aver
by Tri-All arthurs de-cided there,
in sist hyswift in vestiture;
& aye grasp frank,
Albions bulks
thys party-to;
& *howbeit*
re*re*brust w/mighty
yon glowerd
p$_{r}$etty-kings
& barons re*re*filed
counter re*re*bring
wars uncivile fiat –
naetheless
Eldol re-co$_{u}$nciled
en counsel-re-re-forged w/ *Merlin*'nounces
no com*pro*mwisse more:
@ Lammas' next crisping
thys ring pour third round'll re-re-gatherall
for Albions renascence carnivall
& *wort* w\$^{pro}$vision invest
as aArthur pen Dragon
s,ever awaited.

V

~~~~~~~~~~~~~~~~~~~~~~~~~~~~~~~~~~~~

"bmitted their wills, they are obedient to the gods' desires and laws: but at the same time they have d oomed them to death.

'The gods are dying...somewhere in space there are floating, unheard-of corpses...somewhere in sp ace, protracted over centuries and millennia, mons"

–Jean Ray, *Malpertuis.*

"ngali asked his grandfather what they were, t hose dagger birds with long voices. His grandfather saw nothing, heard nothing; the sky was empty; the y did not exist. There was no template in his percep tions for such a thing. And, if some did see somethi ng, then it must be from another world, and theref ore dangerous and best left alone. The magicians h

[. . .]

s. The old man shivered slightly and saw only the c learing with the strangers hurrying back and forth. He saw them because they were men, or creatures in the shape of men."

–B. Catling, *The Vorrh.*

~~~~~~~~~~~~~~~~~~~~~~~~~~~~~~~~~~~~

at the small logging Sæxan outpost-colony of Crow's Lea, one of the mysterious Ladies of the Lakes has appeared near the border of the Forest Perilous, which is being clear-cut for lumber. a A veteran named **Cutha**, *the leader of the local Yaldabaoth Cult, which is rapidly gaining adherents across the Sæxan Shoure and even among brythons, takes it upon himself to face this spectre, and eliminate her: such incidents are occuring throughout the Ængalo-Sæxan colonies.*

The chants of the **C**ult-clan of Cutha, resounding off the rough-hewn wooden walls and rafters of the temple, bite with a frantic edge tonight. The True Sæxons, packed thick within its shadow-bulk, seethe unquiet. They feel, have long felt, the threat of the Others pressing back palpably upon their frontier; and by now this new tale has been whispered from one man to the next, plague-fashion: of the Water-Witch haunting the shunned lake at the Forest-March, of the ghost-harlot recently haunting its waters.

From the ore of Fear, extract the iron of Fury, a precept of Colgrimliche enjoins, and Cutha watches the process before him. Hefty spear-shafts smack on shields, drumming flame-cured wood on flame-cured hide: this is the heartbeat of Yaldabaoth, Onetrue-God, the Death-Compiler, Debt-Collector, Over-man, the One-Who-Is. A hundred hearts beating as one, blade against dead-hide; and a hundred such hundreds are spread all across the Sæxon Shore, and more shall rise when Yaldabaoth declares His war.

Cutha, Lieutenant-Archon of Yaldabaoth and Sub-Chieftain of the Crow's Leah colony, facing his pack, stands rigid as a sword locked in ice. Before him the elite band of Drone-Beasts, their fanatic faces hidden behind their beast-visaged masks, are roaring wildly. The steel-harsh voices of his clan, striking in sharp and rhythmic unison, spark against his flinty glare, growing ever more violent, more thunderous, until, the flame of frenzy struck at last, his ice-stance melts in the heat of their patriotic frenzy. Soon the air within the temple pulses and pricks, hums and buzzes like the innards of a bee-hive shaken – and Cutha's jaw falls open, his lips begin writhing, his tongue begins lurching and flapping within his mouth-cavern, and from its depths booms the voice of Yaldabaoth, snuffing out all other voices:

"Hail Yaldabaoth, the Onetrue God!"

The congregation returns with a hundred throats: *Hail Yaldabaoth, Keeper of the Single Path!*

"Hail he who consumes all that is not Him!"

He is God alone, there is no other but he!

"Hail Colgrimliche, the sword of Yaldabaoth upon earth!"

Hail Colgrimliche, prophet incontestable!

Cutha lets the clan's echoes die against the looming walls, then speaks again.

"Brother-Consumers, Yaldabaoth sees us gathered here!"

We answer the call of the God of Death!

"Hwaet! We are gathered here in Yaldabaoth's timber temple, his mighty Worship-Tomb, made from tree-corpses stacked, felled from the Forest for His pain-slaking, shielded in His fortress from the fickle skies above by solid lumber beams. We feast upon the Forest's beasts, consume its flesh, and gnaw its Wood-meat with our toothsome saws."

The dead wood around them creaks and moans, the sawdust whorls at the Sæxons' feet. "Yet we gather now, goaded by fearsome Forest-terrors rumored, which foment much gall among the natives and among the True Saxons, disquiet."

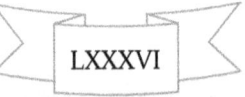

Cutha peers impassive at his people through the temple's gloom, perceives the shifting glance-game playing out there. Thor's Day is a day of industry; only quiet crisis could crowd his clansmen here today. He thinks: *first*, feed them confidence.

"For five-and-twenty years we have fought the Perilous Forest, that dark and dangerous den that spawns mad Brithic tribes, that breeding-bramble of ghouls and wraiths! Twenty-five years – and many are the miles of the Forest's deathfields, countless the acres of groves clear-cut, copious the leveled leahs."

No cheer, no chorus – truly, his tribe is shook. So – best face the fear spear-forward, now. *From iron to ore, from fear to fury.*

"Yet ever, and even as our axes bite deeper, the Forest grows more Perilous. Its paths, like serpent-mazes, twist and curl, contorting, changing course from hour to hour, and week by week our men are lost there. Its leaves rasp harsh from no Real wind, whispering half-seen spectres'curses, hissing in languages enlivened with amorphous lunacy. Its dark depths teem with demons, phantoms, those fiends and gods the aboriginals call *thanes* and *matres*, and other wondrous-weird monstrosities that feed on reason wasted, and seek to unravel all that's Real."

Muffled mutterings amongst the crowd, restive, for Cutha has scraped across a scab; it is not so easy a thing to hear our helpless anxiety given tongue. Audacious, Cutha delves on:

"Mere myths and tales, our leaders tell us! But Yaldabaoth never blinks, as the dead never blink: he sees, as we see, the Forest's alliance with these Brithic savages – how they summon its groves' glamour, how it spurs them to sedition – how they succor its sylvan wounds, how it veils them from vengeance. They shall never labor lamblike, when like wolves they roam the woods. This truth Yaldabaoth sees, as we see!"

More murmuring; they know that Cutha speaks the truth which Baldulf and his cronies will not see. And yet, they do not suspect the half of the horror – not half, for the priesthood know secrets unsensed by the laymen.

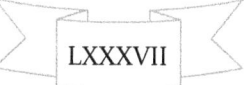

"And Yaldabaoth sees, as we see, that the old gods of our fathers, the gods of the Ængli, the gods of the Sæxons, are paltry here, and powerless! Where was Thor when Hængist, warlord of all the roving Sæxans, was hacked to butcher-bundles by Eldol, the Brithic deity made manifest in battle-blaze?" (*Hear, hear!* bellow the veterans). "Where was Woden when the ghost-king Uther split Hørsa's sternum in fullblown day-blaze, and gutted Octa gullet to groin? Upon this island none have seen our fathers' gods, not once, and yet the fetishes of these primitives slay our leaders and haunt the forest ways. And Wihtgar and Baldulf still persist to call them figments, Brithic follies merely!"

Cutha himself has seen Them, if *see* is quite the word. The World has never healed since that day, when amidst the palpable carnage of the shield-wall, the horror which a Man can slay because it can be seen and smelt and felt and heard and slipped or choked upon, he and a thousand others knew the *absolute rift* that ripped reality itself – a blazing shock of unleashed phantasy that could not be killed, for it lived without existing. He had first felt it merely as a surge, a disturbance in the subtle flux of energies that always flex along the battle-line: a flow of forces physical, mental, emotional, eddies of camraderie and fear and triumph and revulsion that pulse beneath the combat's surface, erupting sometimes into shattered shield-walls. Their thane-priests chanting those lulling cadances, their warriors ululating, savage, in witch-casting patterns – Cutha, war-weary with wounds and fatigue and passion-arrears, had found his senses falling into fragments, peeling away from space into senseless shapes that floated like leaves on a pond-face; like a needle, somehow, the chanting voices threaded through them and drew the world behind them like a string, and everything fell into their weirdling rhythm: the clash and clatter of spears and shields, the flash of swords, the shrieks of gutted men, the warm trickle of sweat and blood. And then, horrific thing: the senseless forms and lines that floated there before his eyes seemed to dance wickedly, foreground and background tugging each detail between them, and it had seemed to Cutha that the rim of his own shield had become the sword of a mounted warrior, the whorled wood lining it seemed a shadowed, awful visage, while the dull glint of the brithic helmet beyond it was a bit of mail-clad shoulder, and a bit of cloud beyond seemed a flashing flint of steel – and so indeed it was now, blinding, and the shapes resolved into a rampaging host of gleaming, flickering figures, terrible and sublime. For a moment Cutha told himself he had lost his reason, for they blocked or reflected the sun from the peripheries of his sight, but vanished when he focused on them, seeping into form again on his vision's edge.

Then he had known he was not mad, but the World had been made so – for the *matres* that could not exist had started slaying Sæxans, and there was slaughter, defeat, and shame. And he had known from that day forward that the gods of his fathers are cowards. So too, now, with the many veterans here, who are barking affirmations.

Cutha has fallen silent, transfixed by this scar of memory, and his congregation waits. But now, he feels the God grip him, kindling his heart with cold fire, filling his lungs with strange winds. His voice now flares up, booming even more brashly.

"The mass of our old gods is a mismatched mess, a nest of trifling impotence! Look not to that mob of squabbling gnomes and titan libertines to crush the natives' mad demon-gods! A sordid flock of hen-wives they, the brain-spawn of our sentimental mothers, too affection-enfeebled to cull the weak among gods, among ideas, among men!"

The womb gives birth to nothing but weakness! The timber walls tremble with the gust of the congregation's refrain, the bawling of a hundred bulls in heat, bristling with proud pugnacity. Cutha's strident voice climbs the peak of their masculine hysteria

"Our old gods are hoardes of woman-spawn, born when women ruled over us as equals, they and their gods breeding and nursing ever new ways, ever more – more difference, more confusions, until our very gods were alien even to us! Some say the Romans of old used to slay all but the hardiest of their offspring – the Romans, who conquered these sinister Brithons. So must we do with our own gods: kill all of them that cannot kill for us! Our grandfathers' fathers grasped firm their stiff spears and toppled the Mother-Rule, they waged wondrous war and made the names of *Sæxon* and *Ængel* frightful to all foriegners; but they left alone this sprawling sacred family of flaccid demigods, pathetic abstract parasites. Yet Yaldabaoth, flesh serpent, the Onetrue-God, is coming! He will consume these false idols, for He is all, and we his members shall chew the meat of murdered gods – Yaldabaoth is coming!"

The children of the Grace-State are the Phallus-Will manifest!

"Yaldabaoth is coming, and his One-World un-mothers!"

Yaldabaoth, the Onetrue-Phallus, is coming!

"Yaldabaoth Autogenes despises all wombs, despises all Others!"

Hail the Stillborn-God, Ever-Same, Pure!

The cult's responses are shooting back at him like clockwork now, automatic, clean of thought, unified in a single voice that thrums with the hatred, fear, confusion, and frustrated hope of a hundred hearts subsumed into this single entity of cold, dead Will – a vast machine of nerve and flesh and rage, of calculation and brutal instinct: a living-dead weapon for Yaldabaoth's war upon the Worlds that never were. They are ready now, and Cutha brings this Will to bear upon the terror on their border, the terror he must shortly face.

"Brothers, within the Perilous Forest everything is myriad, multiple, teeming – too many truths, like hydra-heads spouting, prodigious with unsettled marvels, which lead to no treasures, for none can predict there a margin. Within the Perilous Forest there's no thing familiar – for foliage, fauna, and ground-mould and trail-snakes all shift and shimmer when scrutiny flags, for it writhes with illusions, reflections, shadows, images, echoes, and fragments. Within the Perilous Forest, predict at your peril, for dream-drift and chance hold sway over prudent projection – no profit, then, proffered. Within the Perilous Forest, then, behold the Brithic Madness at its prime: therein they unglue form from thought, and life from being, and *Is* from *Not*, and all the World unravel, to re-weave into spider webs that catch and wrap us up, and suck the sense from us like blood."

Swelled up with the God's audacity, yet chilled by the horrors invoked before it, the clan now stands silent in its sacred lumber-cavern, breath-bated, shirking brain-painted shadows. The logs, carved corpses, lean overhead with sullen groans. Cutha continues.

"Just as mighty Rome once gathered up the roads and tribes and gods of all the earth we know, and drew them to itself, and made itself the Centre; as Rome consumed each and every Other that it met, broke apart each neighbour's folkway-flesh, dissolved it in Empire's stoic iron-gut, to assimilate what's chewed to commerce-cud; as Rome once consumed Albion's living wonder-flesh, digesting living chaos-meat into dead and merchant-worthy goods to flow through Empire's veins, Albion's anarchy dissolved in data-acids; just so, my brothers in Yaldabaoth, our Arch-Archon, Colgrimliche, calls for Unity among all True Ængalo Sæxans in the Onetrue-God!"

The Many are Chaos, the One is True!

"Hail the Death-God, for Death consumes all!"

There is no god but he!

"These natives know well Yaldabaoth's imminence! It's for this they infest the forest edges, flock to the wood-deeps, fomenting foul sedition there. And now–" at last, after so many indirect skirmishes, Cutha strikes from the flank directly at the fear that's mustered here – "Now we hear, this past year, many a weird tale, reports of eerie Water-Witches floating in the wastelands, walking upon waves and casting spells of woe. These sly Lake-Ladies the labourers incite, rallying the savages, and many an Ængal, on sight, they've driven mad, and many a Saxon, at a word, they have unmanned. And now at last–" A thrill or chill shivers through the hall – "by three of our number has such a creature now been seen, right here upon our own frontier, the pond just past the Place of Crows, and there she menaces our axe-men."

Indeed, one of the three had come back mad, grasped by lunacy, as crazed as any Brithon. But he had not been a believer. Cutha feels a grim, soundless groan deep within his glacial being, yet his icy surface remains hard, still, uncracked. He draws a breath.

"Hwæt: Baldulf-Wispbeard with his shield-walls will not face the Forest-Wraiths; nay, he laughs away as merely nightmare the wicked things that mangle us! Nor will the priests of Woden smite the Forest-Wights; oh, no, their limp-hung totems leave them languid before the Brithic phantoms! Hwæt: it is Yaldabaoth who shall crush this chaos-breeder, it is His True Sæxans who shall slay this sedition-mare, it is I, his sub-archon, a fist of the One, who shall battle this anarch-bitch, armed with the Spear of the Still-born God!"

And the lumber-throated chapel rings with his cult-clan's bellowing, boots bashing planks, spearhafts hitting hide. The fury is on them, a hundred True Saxons howling like the sea-storm, and Cutha floats on their froth of vengeance-pride; a swimmer in this ocean or oracle, his arms flung wide, he dives into prayer:

"We praise you, Father of the Dead Earth, Yaldabaoth!
We praise you, Father through a father only!
We praise you, god of the grave-face impassive!
We praise you, god of the barrow-coin!"

You are God, there is no other but thee!

"Let us revile, o Body-Rot-God, what sense won't reveal!
Let us crush, o God with your Arrow-Head-Crown, all chaos!
Let us annihilate, o Corpse-Cold-God, all anarchy!
Let us murder, o Matter-Bound God, what will not be measured!"

You are God, there is no other but thee!

"We praise you, Yaldabaoth, for you are perfect, One!
We praise your prophet holy Colgrimliche, who is perfect through you!
My people praise me, your priest Cutha, purified with pagan blood-gulp!

We praise you, Triple-Male, in perfect singularity!
You are God, there is no other but thee!
"Bless us, Yaldabaoth, as the dead are blessed, we Saxons True!
Blissful order, stasis, surety we seek from you!
Bless our sap-slaked axes, charm our saws that chew upon tree-tissue!
Bless us, True ÆngaloSæxans, & cleave the heathen heresiarchs in two!
The Many are Chaos, the One is True!
"Your curse on Brithic hosts and ghosts!
Your curse on their new-whelped Arthur, wraith-boy-king!
Your curse on Anna, princess girlie-ghoul, if not falsehood be the brat!
Your curse on the Forest of Demons, phantastic fortress of our foes!
The Many are Chaos, the One is True!
"Hwæt, Yaldabaoth! I am your vengeful instrument!
Make me your muscle to smite the Water-Witch!
Make me dead to all but the State of grace!
Make me your blade to part her spectral viscera!
Make me dead to all but duty done!
Make me your ire that blinds her eyes with fire!
Make me dead to all but the draw of death!
Make me your nail to peel her skin away!
Make me dead to all but the calm of decay!
Make me your tooth to dig within her!
Make me dead to all but what's dust and clay!
Make me your tongue to lick up her ichor!
Make me dead to all but entropy's law!
Make me your gullet to swallow her flesh!
Make me dead to all but the glory of flesh!
Make me your gut that death dissolves to death!
For armed in Yaldabaoth's flesh, I go to slay the Lake-Wraith-Lady!"
And now his cult-clan's chorus erupts,
concise with sacred cruelty: *Blood! Blood! Blood!*

And grimly, Cutha grabs his cloak, he thrusts aloft his priestly scepter-sword; swallowing a throng of ghostly terrors, he strides through his howling adept-horde, parting them like water, and flings the grumbling gate wide.

He steps outside, and the ecstasy falls from him like a dead limb. Inside the temple's shadow, everything is always focused, simple, clear; outside here beneath the sky, where everything squirms with contradictory life, contingency still rules; otherness is everywhere. But – *Weakness, hidden, withers away*, says Colgrimliche. So Cutha measures his steps, forbidding his pace to betray his apprehension through either haste or hesitation; he feels his people's eyes upon him, seeking the God's divinity within, doubt and fanaticism flickering within them like tongues of fire. He strides on mechanically, letting their gaze slip from him like spent sword-blows from a buckler.

Trailed by his pack, Cutha passes the dark hulk of the temple's armory, where hammer-blows still ring out against the dead-muffled air despite the day's menace, or perhaps because of it. Otherwise, a sickly silence stretches between the stockade's wooden walls, a withholding of breath, like a deathbed-heave. He nears the gate's yawning jaws, surmounted by a tangle of antlers snapped from the skulls of Forest-flushed deer, and, muttering a prayer to Yaldabaoth, walks through it, leaving the compound behind him.

As always, the eternal Cloud stretches grim and grey above, its jaundice-dirt aura muddling itself into the distant, muted hulks of the colony, whose jagged silhouette is piled around the profile of Woden's temple. The Cloud is formed from the ash and smoke of Hængist's great Tower, burned by the Brithons' pen-Dragon god Ambrosius over a dozen years ago, and from its particles, says Colgrimliche, the Stillborn-God has composed his body. Yet Yaldabaoth's barrow-house is not welcome within the town's stockade, so Cutha's clan has declared their claim here, midway between the town and the lumber-camps on the Forest-Shore, toward which he now directs his steps.

He need not turn round to be sure his folk still follow him, though he knows they will drop off little by little as he nears the Lake. They are devout, his people, but prey to all the false distractions and phantasmic notions wafted out on the Forest breeze or on Brithic tongues or from the priestly miasma of the sick-house of the old gods; and as each of his followers drops away, he will mark his tipping-point between faith and fear. But – *From the ore of Fear, extract the iron of Fury.* Cutha will face this Water-Witch, whatever subtle magic she deploys, and through him Yaldabaoth will extinguish her demonic sway. His Drone-Beasts will behold the triumph, replay the tale for his loyal clan, and their sinews will swell with Yaldabaoth's sovereignty; Colgrimliche, too, will hear of it, and Sub-Archon Cutha shall be a name the Leader will not forget.

Cutha comprehends his people's fears; the path to perfect certainty is long and fraught. He himself had wandered several years, unmoored upon the earth, as if the hole in the World-That-Is still gaped there before him, a gap torn out of the Real, bleeding madness, sucking him slowly in. The old gods were dead to him; the only ones he knew could act upon the world, were those that were impossible, and did not even claim to *be* – and they were the evocations of his Enemy. Indeed, among the many outlandish sects and uncanny systems which, in his desperate search, he had picked up and discarded, he had briefly flirted even with the Brithic gods themselves, inquired of his workers about their *thanes* and *matres*, and spoken to their thane-witch-priests. But it has long been known that the natives' madness is contagious, and he could not tolerate these primitive savages speaking in broken nonsense, in an insolent language without rule or order, made more of chokes and stutters than of words serving *things*. He learned only that the Brithic Madness and the Brithic Magic could not be pried apart, and must be destroyed together. At last he had heard of the prophet Colgrimliche, the visions bestowed upon him, premonitions of Ængalo-Sæxan power, pride, and vengeance; he had sought him out, seen him preach, and on that day Yaldabaoth had claimed Cutha's will forever as His own. The Sæxans would be great again. Yet even then, there would be years of futile questioning and faltering resolve before the Stillborn-God walked and spoke through him; and these, his clan, are mostly simple people, their skulls packed more with thoughts of loss and profit than with dreams of dying gods.

This loss and profit issue from the lumber yard, which he now finds stalled, haunted by awkward gawking labourers clumped at intervals against their low, long barrack walls and in the shadows of stacked-log-mountains. The workers are mostly young Brithic serfs whose restricted rations and rights are augmented if they volunteer for this arduous duty, shunned by their fellow, Forest-bred natives. Certified by Baldulf's regime as 'Civilised Brithons', such men dress in the Sæxan fashion and speak in the Sæxan tongue – at least around their masters – and worship the old, castrated Sæxan gods – at least around their masters; and for each primitive practice they abandon, their leash is lengthened a little longer, and flaked with a bit more fool's-gold; for Baldulf wants workers, and the Sæxans are too proud for peaceful labour.

Colgrimliche has denounced this pandering, and calls to crush their culture now, at spear-point, for no more can a Brithon wrapped in a Sæxan cloak become a Sæxan, than a stick of wood become a sword with a shred of foil wrapped around it. Sæxan spies are as vigilant as ever, lists of troublers at the ready, and another Night of Long Knives would make more docile Brithons than false promises of freedom will ever do. And indeed, Cutha detects no Sæxan loyalty in these loungers, feigning fear with a smirk and a yawn. But the little band of Sæxan woodsmen, men of firmer mettle, are also huddled here, and truly scared they scurry to the priest when he appears, deflecting indignity like darts with their crazed gesticulations and tales of feminine horror-magic. The colony's war-band, dispatched by its chieftain Oslaf, whose personal absence is loud, also cowers in a demoralised crowd around the till-gate, their eyes shame-shifting, cowed by the glamour of the Water-Witch. At last Cutha turns his head – slowly, regally, like a chieftain surveying his army – and sees that indeed, over half his pack has now abandoned him, scattered in his rear, watching from a distance; the rest shuffle on, trepidation shimmering through them.

Oslaf will soon lose his post if not his head, thinks Cutha, for the whole operation here has surrendered to terror. Every day for the last three years, ten hectares of timber has been felled by axes, decapitated, vivisected with saws, and heaved onto miles-long cart-caravans, hauled either across the Sæxan Shore for stout fort-walls and war machines, or else shipped across the seas in trade for gold and grain and steel and implements of combat. The refugee creatures fleeing the axes, when they do not escape into the Forest's depths, are shot in the skies or the stump-studded fields, butchered where they fall, their skins flesh-peeled, their flesh bone-peeled, and all is consumed: eaten, worn, tanned, ground up, sold. Every hour wasted here is a crate of gold drained from the colony's coffers. Very well, thinks Cutha; if Oslaf intends to let this wealth slip through our fingers, let the priest of Yaldabaoth catch it, and let all take note.

The remains of his retinue are slowing sheepishly to a halt behind him, dread-scuttled on the Forest's tidal shore, his retinue dwindling as he forces himself on, his boots sinking in the soft morass of mud and uprooted grass, criss-crossed with mounded tracks of dragged tree-carcasses, scattered with the giant husks of trees sunk into the mud like beached wood-whales, picking his way round jagged stumps thrust up like hoary graves. More of his people abandon him at the dark peninsula of woods known as the Crow's Leah, from which the colony takes its name – a curved arm of the Forest arcing around the eastern shore of the lake it still screens, and defended by a populous rook of monstrous warrior-crows who tenaciously attack, with savage violence, every work party sent to level it, so that the forest has been chipped around it, leaving the Leah intact and dangerous.

There, he finds a straggling encampment of several dozen vagabond natives, some preparing scraps of scavenged food or mending scraps of clothing, others minding their young, or singing or playing at games or scratching their runes on sheaves of bark – for paper is forbidden to the workers and serfs, except those certified as *Civilised* – others simply sprawled beneath tattered tents, lost in delirium or dream.

There are always a few such renegades clinging to the Forest's shrinking margins, but their numbers have swelled, proof for his warning that this spectral Lady is swift becoming a touchstone of sedition. For a year Cutha's superior, Archon Æthelbryht of Sussex, has forwarded reports from spies and drones sent deep into the Forest, sealed for Cutha's eyes only. Each month, not scores but hundreds of the Brithons take refuge there, a steady, unseen stream of runaways, refugees, heretics and rebels. Its perilous groves hide secret libraries, fortresses, schools, even farmsteads. The regime estimates the count well into the thousands, excluding the mere women and whelps: a veritable army of vengeful lunatics, mystics, magicians, and insurgents, should any crafty Brithon – this Arthur, for instance – manage to muster them. And some report rumours that Anna, his mysterious co-regent never yet spotted, is even now scouring the Forest for just this purpose. Plenty mock this absent girlie-queen as weaker even, surely, than her pipsqueak sibling, just thirteen; but Cutha is more circumspect, for he knows that the witchery of women, in their weakness, is most wicked.

The air has grown oppressive, as if the Cloud above were a leaden cloak, while the wind above has whipped into a whining, wild keen, and a wet electric prickling creeps along the Sæxans' skin. When he orders the camp dispersed and its chattel-folk detained, the remainder of his followers are quick to seize the excuse to extract themselves. With the butts of their spears they lay into the vagrants with violent gratification, avenging their humiliating fear upon the cringing, shouting refugees, ripping apart their tent-hovels and setting them aflame, as if these were images of their own persistent cowardice in the face of native magic; then they hastily herd their prisoners back toward the lumber-yard and away from the dreaded Lake.

Meanwhile Cutha paces along the edge of the Leah, toward its extremity, now followed only by his guard of a half-dozen Drone-Beasts. Even these stolid, veteran berserkers of Yaldabaoth are treading gingerly, their knuckles pale-gripped upon their spears, each peering with wide eyes from a helm hung with the skin of a beast he has slain, on whose blood he has slaked: a fox, a stag, a bear, a boar, a wolf, a savage-cat.

By the time they round the long copse's tip and the Lake's broad steely surface glimmers at them from a nest of mist, even the guard falters, and he proceeds alone, a painful bubble of panic swelling in his chest, bulging against his ribs, forcing itself up through his gullet as his legs keep marching on, traitorous and mechanical, through the tall grasses that whip against his calves, toward the womb of singing water swathed in sheets of glaring trees. Cutha wants to flee. He is feeling it again – he knows this frisson, he senses the shifting. He does not want what is about to occur.

Suddenly he does not want to be the fist of Yaldabaoth, he does not want to face the rift of stoic Reason once again, he does not want to gamble his mind on a self-aborted god, and breathless, ashamed, he is blubbering pleas and recantations under his breath, spitting his faith out from his frantic mouth. It is futile. He has given his will to Yaldabaoth, and it is his own no longer. A pawn emptied of faith, subject to mere belief, Cutha watches himself drawn forward, and another shift occurs within him. He is swept by the calm of the dying – the sweet abjection of hope renounced, the cold solace in the imminent, final, eternal spasm, the horizon beyond which it will all never have mattered, never occurred. Cutha is staring into Yaldabaoth's dead-filmed eyes.

But they are not only that – for he sees now that they are his own eyes as well, filmed like those of frogs or fish, and that his face is dry and shriveled, or perhaps moist and wrinkled, and writhes upon his skull like thin paper agitated by a colony of maggots squirming beneath it. It is floating, flattened like a mask, as if upon the surface of a pond; and some part of him is tugging at himself, and whispers that he has reached the shore of the haunted Lake, that he has fallen to his knees – in prayer? in shock-sickness? in agony? in preparation for an axe-blade on his nape? – and it is his own reflection waving there beneath him. He reminds his self that he is Cutha, fist of Yaldab...but now, he sees that a hand he's got is reaching, trailed by a tattooed arm that is his own, grasping at the image of his self there in the water, through the curls of mist that grasp at him, at his arm, cool upon his skin. Yes, he is reaching toward his self there in the water, slowly, fearfully. He touches him, and sees his self touch him, watches his self gaping at him, gulping fishlike. His self is struggling to form stumbling soundless words, its lips stretching and bending weirdly, silent and staring, waving its arms in mysterious and impossible gesticulations.

Cutha is sure his self is drowning, but he too is gulping now, the air burning in his lungs like water, two palms slapping on the silty mud like flopping fish; he watches the panic on his self's face as its orifices stretch and tremble, the skin-flesh around them distorts and ripples, fragmenting into jostling shapes and colour-smears in which his self dissolves. A pathetic moan escapes a mouth that is his, and he struggles to tug back the drifting patches into a semblance of a face – and so he does: a scintillating visage flickering through glances and glints of refracted light, a collage of image and immanence – it is a mournful moon cast upon the pond-glass, a will o' the wisp given frail mortal form, a pale phosphorescent algae floating just beneath the murk, the waxen skin of a water-nymph adrift in endless sleep. She is emerging now, floating upward toward the brackish Cloud above, the Lake's surface clinging to her like a sheet of silk, a mounded film that stretches over her head and her shoulders as she rises, and then in a spasm of release reverts to liquid, sluicing back down along her graceful form in moist-dusty diamonds of fluid light. Her form, it seems, is nothing but that stream of sheeted gleaming, though the ghosts of colour somehow still linger on her body where they had never been at all. He cowers, he feels muscles trapped inside the body he is wearing, and they are twitching, spasming, striving to escape it.

He is struck through with awe, as a blade of light slices through the Cloud above her, a fountainhead of illumination pouring through like honey-water from a punctured flask, flowing over her, tossed back up from the rippling waters and glowing mists, above which she now floats in cascades of kaleidoscopic spray, her hair waving in silky tentacles about her, the air alive with a million minuscule fluid droplets each tossing off a hundred reflected rays. The darkling Forest, the iron Cloud, the glassy Lake, the luminous Lady, the lambent fog, all buzz with an aching, lovely intensity that burns away all colour and all thought, a blaze of radiance that vaporizes all distinction, incinerating the horizon; he is bathed in this liquid surge, a mouth upon his face gasps wide in surprise and he is flooded with it, choked.

Above him, amidst a corona of blinding effulgence, poised upon a mist of tears, She smiles, and a certain terror plummets out of him, like an anchor cut; giddily he seems to shoot toward some internal surface, noticing at last that the pain-dread has been shed from him, that the light does not sear him, but washes his skin like fresh water. Yet he feels within him a new thing, growing – whether flesh-thing or mind-thing he cannot decide – at first in the cavities where the old fear had crouched, but then pressing or seeking a space in his nerves or his flesh or his dreams or his gut, a dim hungry outcast returned to its estate after countless years, and vainly seeking the rooms it once haunted, finding only strangers.

He is sucked up in the tide-pool of an aching and absent desire; he ventures to name it, grasps at it, loses, is swept out to some Sea deep within him, where its object dissolves among the currents; he is rocked by strange swelling waves of ecstatic despair, and wrapped in warm swaths of a burgeoning and ludic prescience; and suddenly the recognition washes over him: this is Beauty.

His vision refocuses upon the Lady floating there above, and she is not dark, but beautiful and terrible as the Morning and the Night, beguiling as the Sea and Sun and Snow upon the Mountain, ravishing and dreadful as the Storm and the Lightning. She is a cataract of glory, a rush of Beauty that splinters every craft upon the stones of reality slicing the eddies: her form ever retreating from his delirious gaze, detail lost in its own contradictory multiplication, kaleidoscopic, over-lain, over-drawn, over-written, over-wrought, She is a Beauty like water – invisible, formless and flowing, cleansing and nourishing, light-loving, renewing, and made for humankind to drown in. All shall love her, and all shall despair, for the dreams she promises have flown past before we even wish them.

For a moment he glimpses, in the Lake's silty depths, the fish-nibbled body of a bloated, Stillborn Thing; then his thought flows away.

The Lake is singing now, a reverberant crystal-song, as if intoned in mournful chorus by cicadas carved from ice. It uses Her mouth, and the mouth that he has too, and he is startled to discover, like a worm in his throat, his own voice. A final vestige of something called Cutha is plucking his thought, and he struggles haphazardly to carve himself away from what is transpiring here – painfully, sorrowfully hooking and piercing the parts of him, pulling together his self. A will that is acting within him grasps his jaw, his lips, his tongue; it grips his throat and grabs his lungs, and against the growing chaos of light and song and passion, his mouth like a dying gasp is made to ask, rasping against the delicate air: "Who are you, witch?!"

And a fountain of laughter springs forth from her mouth, gushes in peals of ominous mirth that threaten to drown him. His self's frail craft, lashed so crudely together, is swamped for good, its flotsam scattered in her outburst's uproarious storm. The laughter continues – too long, too long, or perhaps it is weeping; and its stutters and gasps are too measured, repeating, they're stumbling in loops, a laughter-chant sobbing, and all around it's raining light and laughter.

He looks up, sees a mouth on her straining and stretching, a tar-black abyss, and a horror-bliss seizes him: for a soul is flowing out from it, leaking, simply streaming through the lips, like a Graal overflowing. Then those lips, as her voice flows forth, gape wide – fine teeth meet against her tongue – she gapes again, in mirrored mouth-form:

“AИNA”

The Drone-Beasts wait, apprehensive, sullen and silent, on the far side of the Crow's Leah, none mentioning the tacit retreat from sight of the Lake, which had played out, without any conscious decision, while their leader had pressed on. It is not until long after the spectral cacophony of sound and ghostly light has ceased to rebound from the Cloud above, as the eventide sun is engulfed by the Forest-Sea, that Sub-Archon Cutha finally returns. His gait is listless and stumbling, and he sways and bobs like the mast of a pinnace on restive waters. Belatedly emboldened, the Drones creep out to meet him.

Instinctively they spread out as they approach him, as if bringing a boar to ground or running down a captive. Their priest halts his meandering trudge some ten paces from his chain of men; instinctively, as if he had given an order, they do the same. An unnerving silence reigns, and Cutha's face, backlit by the setting sun, hides in inscrutable shadow. The captain, Cæwlin in his tattered boar-mask, takes one, then two tentative steps forward, then advances farther, til his raised palm blocks the dying light's obscuring glare.

Cutha's eyes are dull and filmy, like those of a fish, or a stillborn corpse.

VI

~~~~~~~~~~~~~~~~~~~~~~~~~~~~~~~~~~~~

"sleeper has awakene"

– Herbert, *Dune.*

"range women lying in ponds distributing s words is no basis for a system of gover"

– *Monty Python and the Holy Grail.*

~~~~~~~~~~~~~~~~~~~~~~~~~~~~~~~~~~~~

folk flock from all Albion to the ceremony of confirmation and investiture at Ynys Wydryn, the Island of Glass – a hill in the centre of a vast floodplain, which at high tide becomes an island connected to land by one narrow causeway. it is preceded by three days of carnival and social intensity, in which the merging passions of all Albion forge subliminal bonds amongst each other and with the new pen-Dragon, charging & investing **arthur** *withal.* **the Ladie of Lakes**, *hitherto known only in rumour, makes her appearance at last. during the traditional hazing of the new pen-Dragon,* **Lot** *declares his contempt for arthur and refuses his ascendency. the Ladie disparages both as warmongers, revealing that she possesses Caliburn, s'word of Albion, and thus will ultimately decide who is worthy of it; the path, she says, is not through war howbeit, Lot's followers and the robber-barons withdraw to gather an army against arthur, while arthur's supporters confirm him as provisional pen-Dragon, establish a court, and prepare for war.*

!th'Invest'ure-Fest 'tis **F**raught

w/fr*an*xt*ic*ous exhubliss, oniero'man ic glee
+scab-barded s'words, irony-forged
ill-temper'd ayebut ,bite^barb*d*
:so this balmy lammas finds eht g*id*difickly albrithons
bubbling brethren-close: both 'lation and loawthe
boil the hill-bowl in neweteb eht banks
d'Ynys Wydryn's glass-îsle pillarpit –
matres&brythons amass't on'th'beaches
)cl'nchd r'nd th'bay(
:all floodbound at tideswell 'cept sole ~~cause~~way slimtip'd barelie surface'pon:
=> centerisen isle-tor , Avalon*s*entry-point
:*Ynys Wydryn*:
Pillar albionic ,rect o'er
Pit o'liquid mirror avalonic;
Pen- prop oetical of perméant dream–poised o'er

Pannier of Ink–wells up w/th'moon-drag on;
Parlaimeant of th'folk Albrithic
Perch of pen'Dragons, place
wherein with th'Albrithons' h*arm*ony
arthur's immanence'll be invested
d*re*emed pen-Dragon his *mailed* arm shall be
the strength of Albion his crafty *crown* shall be
the will of Albion, ere three-days carnival's out-caroused.

in friendly flocks or w'aspish, the **P**halansteries[7]
h'orison-sp'read glid *la*n*g*q*uid* o'er the hill-surfs
folk-&-c,art-flows merry, floes drift of pr*air*ie-sailing archi*tent*ure,
b*road*wheeld acre-*plan*ted t*run*dle-*garde*ns rumbling-on
s'w*arm*ed about *w/w*alksong –
tightdrawn tugdanced toward the Tor togæther til
each eddied in wigglicourse intimate pressurized torrent
boistrous~*mot*ley~ r f r action~mosaïc~naîtrous~albion~r'ush ers
to fix in manifest ; ô *arthur* to fix within themselven Albion to manifest ; ô
*!Lo=> ava*u*nt* the *joyous-garde* of Cærleon roules by
bedew'd in deck'd of myriad mottlied hue
–,see w art*hur's* tnallag retinue
ensconced in sterical hue & crye
of Albion's fair i e mab-mob merry ,aye;
& arthur himselven on chariot rides
tugged two cheerly druggar-beste bears by
from Per'lous Forest hied;
mais too w art*hur's* doughty-fortified by keen cold eyes
of eager knives @waist
in-circled'sunbroken,of:*Bedwyn+Brastias+Ector+Cador+Caï*:orbit,of≈*arthur*;
howbeit how haopey their laughter –

7 attending in entire *corpus civitas* (pro,claims un armorican tome) we find (in excess of pen-Dragon-led Cærleon): Tintagel , Fawllmouth [née Terrible] , Exeter , Totnes , Carmarthen , Cardif , Isca , Notteng , Hull , Cadbur , Lanark , Petreloo & Londinium ;+ aussi many cenacles, families, & singularities; so too in tendtance note Benoic's Riothamus + Gorre's Uriens; also myriad ambassadors in avatar towhit: come-of-Fidelme&Gilloman of the Gæls , & others come-of-the Gauls et come-of-the-Pictes.

&*!Lo*=> a doublembassy from hybrid Gore descendts:
1.) eht retinue d'*Uriens& Rovæna* in friendly form & office
2.) *Lot*'s *lack*eyes: half loud & lowering/half(&Lot themselven)silent & stone
& nigh five fathoms' grass*s*ea cleaves their columns –
&aussi;b,rash the robber-barons' warbands(spearbutts-up in peaceoath)
bash like boat-p,rows athwaort the briny hu'manic billows –
...} "ô : how might'lie power's augerèd, so many erst
wh'île-enemies hence
hied for lying
arms down for arthur*!...*" – {...

&Lô-of-Lôs!=> a finely mist upon the skin
of Ynys Wydyrn's sur,face lucid
whoirlslinking *Cloud* ref*l*iction
dampelectringles all
th'host rimm'd liquid round eht
glass – looking
focus'd albrithionic gaze
likeunto tulpic sunrays =>
tide backw*is*eeps running
&mudsuckslow's tugg'd
water slurp'd-up gulp'd by sea-maw
cho*c*ked with fog-tongue cotton seeming
all in vapourdown dissolved~~et leaving
drublen upfrom muckfloor's midst reveal'd
stilm et tall un figurement of lumiant glory
coolblaze astral shimmerthrue
thrushing thrilly Ynys Wydyrn's airnerve
:'tis un *Lady* terribilic *of Waters* risen
~~&~ripples~thru~atom*waves*thought*waves*~irradiant~cast~~
acrost et tidelandbay
her hair darkdrifting liketo sea-grass
eyes blown of suboceovolcanic glass:
the *Ladie of the Lakes* has come at last
,scended to Albion 'sembled.
graciouslie thys Ladie's*m*île
few her limpid word-waves

Brastias
b,uckle-knee'd
b'rindl,es full ashen
,beshrinketh him

; yet still her deeply murks unplumb'd &
each conc[w]ise reply's
spill'd through like liquid phrases &
insists: *as Witness ,alone, tis she visits* *+ her acolyte*
,{for presentbide}...
;yet Merlin's eyes
hide laçitian suspicions
+ intimate filiations infrathin
, as if'twere rip-tides 'twixt her lips
, as if'twere a prodigiosity
unth'ought.

anon:

3 Days≈> *gâmes · p,ark'd-gardens · orchestras · feasts · recitatives · debates · theatricals · dances · dérives · exhibits · oratories · contests · libraries · griotsongs · prayers · intoxications · ecstasies in mass:*
3 Days' ludic disjunct mindthrob whirlpool
hyperculture festcollage , pluricommunal
kaleidoscopic madnessyzygy of Albion's myriads
ineffable agapē of play
blooming presubidealic bond-roots drink deep
of springs & rains of fluidifférence
which bonds–so rooted–bonded will
arthur to all ,upon the final triad, be.

so ;– 'twas ever the **R**ite on some unplann'd hour
for th'albrithons to mock t'heir pre-Pen-Dragon's ~~power~~
re-mind them t'heir might 's but farts of moist brains
– launching spitballs a-hock ,raunchy jabs, punding names
,at t'heir avatar-elect & mongst nonsensic hazing drizzles
sertayne jibes with craft inflect valid grievance spoke in missials.
thus'twas pon the path of *arthur* stands *Lot*;

all yon henchlings *Lot* hath call wort[8] « *younglyng* & *sot* »
« *yawling-babe, hœlpless whelp,* » « Merlin's *plaything, craven dolt,* »
« *drit-cherl, dumbhick swamp'yond aide, dummy-King of Fools-gold* »
& suchlike epithets; *Lot* themself their jaws un-locks, their lungs
upumpassing well, and joins the troast, their brazen voice out wrung:

“

Lot: hwæt, lad! well met – de,spite thine earen wetted yet;
oo, « *!!!h'ail h'ail!!!* » tho I ne'er know-me *if* ye're hale
aye in *deed* thou'rt scarce gold-vetted:–
truebetold I nae have known thee aye correctlie:
untrue-tried in hardistance
untrue-tried in commoun weal
untrue-tried in wisdumbattle
untrue-tried in ought'cept c,la mes
long-dissolved authority –

pup,pet > than person

massk > than matre

thra ll > than thane –

cause scarcenough port'ends=>*me*
if sooth or nae that *Uthers* & *Ygraine's* brat ye be;
not by bloodline's Albion drawn:
here end these heredit y ed heads! « *!! hear hear, here here !!* »
Nay, nae leader ye, tho ye *af,firm* Lot's *congreg'ants*
trot in ensconced in rabbling-mobs *& many more aside in cline*
a motley foolcrowd sorbed in solip *& scarce e'en list their dis*
phant*ass*enine mess sap *-course further to*
p'd o' compass or correct'ion, *as them applaudited & lauded*
free rei g n of contra,diction t'angled, madly mixed
anarchaos ,cross'd op'pinions cross'd impureposes
,a l*un*atic fabric w,oven all of f*ring*e!

---

8 *wort*: dead ~~n'âme~~ of *arthur*

hwæt ye kid:[9]

nae suchwisse shall ye seek the Social Path correct,
by flaunt of firmtrue Fact; o nae!
see: dialectic => reSolution!
from many (for many = error) bl'end => few => one :correct;
now b'end be ,for the Sin,gle T'ruth!
ne *we* nor *us* may be if thererror be *I* \&/ *thee,*
nor none misagree but be mine enemy;
mark well ,yclluckling child;
mine eyes besotted w/futurity
all rays've prismfilter'd, similated
cause I say truthily:

"
the One Correct Way lies thru me!

whereupon *arthurs* bec ,louded his **V**y'sage
like f,ireboltlight sparcks his eyen à fl'âme-beam
emanant avec impendant pluroma ,tis
utter with subl*i'mage* ,awe-full as rain-bow, & d'arts
he passionates forth en retort:

arthur: "**H**ydra qwest *h*vaunting *laughs* honey, thesauri,
laughs v,ector *mis*prison, *laughs* y'ester @ wax
yr um,pyre-frisson, *laughs* nest'or-thumb out
for myrmid,on wave'rs sea-fickle vec our vively *laughs*
eclecstattic quest association, beast decentral *laughs*
ne ~~ban~~'dead *laughs* yr jackboot mogenous reflects
lô our inæternal *temp*er'*d* airy autonomen
lô our affinfinity at'tr,action zone in
mutual *laughs* our phalanstatic versity in

9 ...member thee *Lot* but a few off-digits be from *arthur's* years...

*un*expect et e*verve*nture a*id*e
mine acephaleic *laughs*
at all yr *Lot!*"

:this the mouth of *arthur* **U**tters, uther'son
;but *laughs* none come from
Cador, Benoic's brash spring-son
b'lushed lofty avec burndish choler
sputters ,roundbout casts hot glares
,hooksnags pon power watching – pon her calls :

Cador: "**A**vaunt's ô Liquid's Lady gazing's ,glayz'd
et languid's, let yr words assuayge
thys vyle's *Lot*'s so t*empty*ous out'srage –
affyrm ye fayre's *arthur's* legitimance re-solved's!"

mais the ***Ladie of Lakes*** grimnes mere;
anon melodic she rivulets otni res*pond*se:

"leave aslide , so-ga*un*tle men , **P**reeninpuffry ,an ye may;
scarce i pleasaunce sip im,posed in power,
& leave unto cæsar cæsar's Dis:ease.
what s'ways adjure i b,rush ne bi'nary beaches
à ne State s'wells my tiding;
nor no,ble fighting ; *form just peace,*
young t,*ago*nists , ere aide or heed be*sea*rch me.
in,fluence fluid's , ne f*or*ce n*or* fo*r*m , my potendancy-flow;
in'direct , ion's d'rift my fa'cult *ys* tinctsure;
in diffused permeations , mixed mists of seep;
in visible laps of sleep , rare*sigh*ted but in gnitfihs rainstrands;
myne fav'our you scarce
*sh*all myne as know
but pon yr own glass'd face bestow.

;*howbeit* – whilst earbent-ye . . . tis not it be so, ye boys,
thys treas~~ure~~d s'word from anv il d rag'd's
no dragon's blade – tis co*un*ter*feit* !, i ken:
for Caliburn (gainst vile dnespotism
vouchsafed) s'vanishd – nor aughtt'account for it?
well : let's be told a thing thee , then:
pour thys very *Brastias* now afore me bow'd,
'bove a dozen of yearly ago before me bow'd;
he bore *right* elbow crook-in a beam'd et babblic babie,
he lifted *left* longsheening a pen-dant s'word , keen blade
of pen-Dragons – {at last yea ,syr *Brastias*, may
yr floodgate unlip!} – so ,all ye boys, well-list:
?brag ye a s'tone-wrenchd s'word? : ¡pen-Dragons'word ,thee *none*!
?*arthur* boast ye ap uther? : ¡*anna* thee *none* ap morgygraine!
the s'Word'Albion scends to whoso't *earns* its pen-
when her epoch is come appears dragon-anna yr friend –
et aft muchel'r lab'our occultly all's ready well done.
on *ce* moment , howbeit , two brats*h*-boys monal 's'all *i* mark:

to sordid hierarclash I leave ye; mais –"
(her words steam *her* voice spring-dew *her* eyes icicles *her)*

– "mark *ye*:

whome'er leastlose thystruggle for y'our yearn,
muchel penance *muchel* proof *muchel* metamorpheus
must obstac*all* thy path ere merit Caliburn;
pour," *hereat she straungelie smiles , dulgent , g'lancing ,* "passing
on of s'words tis ne patent-hold of *Merlin*."

her dis'courses thus her, voice of ripple ring'ing
rain-dainty, & the p'ending course polightly she awaits

Brastias
blancheth

avec her sigh-lent
acolyte

straightaway sp*lit*h'under **S**h*cra*c*K*tters carniv,all

à chaos tossd in ,*sudd*sp'rung dread, w/panick pelted

,eht tsepmet C'loud oer brythains -bursts

& tricely lo 1 score

o' passion-tractional-phalanxii => phalanxii o'war.

two camps re-~~treat~~

pour e ther

bi nary a gain.

range d in vective **D**eafiance again,st

th'ascent of un'ætheling *arthur*, foes as*sembl*ed:

muchel hordes cleave *Lot's* cult of orderlie Gore unto:

thousandes @ his father *Uriens'* ambi-valent muster,

+ *Nentres*' brelding band Goreswell'd yet further;

+ th'*Carados* clan + folk o'*morgAnor:* all *Lot's* m'arching muscle.

+1pack of Pictes to'em r'ally, chiefed by *Talorc*, petty p,ain't-princeling.

nor *Lot's* camp monopolis is; be,yon' his spell

join di, verse ssidents be-sides:

cf. th'albrithionic mechanick-cenacle of

Clariance + e'en eht

Yaldabaoth-cult of ængelosæxan *Ægwissance* etc.

nor fold yr earen yet: for doubly-nigh

t'heir numbers<= robber-barons huffingly inflate

,in greed togathren-bonded hight th': "***Corporation of Barons***"

viz: g'rifting-band of baron *Crandallmas*

+ *Idres*, savage baroness avec her gla*u*ditory drones

+ duke de *Caudebennett's* cohort, called

by cow'ring pauvres: *No-Bo*'*y of Bernicia*

+ pettimany other all staravening for fight

their leashes grasped in gaunt,let hand

their chief of chiefs, noToryous baron
all commands, yclept "th'
-king w/100 cNights".[10]

to *arthur* en plen*tie* **P**ledge autres, towit:

his ~~un~~-kin *Cai&Ector* plus his Cærnish clan
,Brastias captaining; hys
eld'ers *Eldol led by, & Merlin*(mirrorkin) mystering sly;
eke numbrous phalanxes flecting *All*bion,
eke @*Lœdegrants*' gift :a landed grain armada
,devestration-army's laden grand phalanstery-feeder;
& myriad youth pour taleworth posterity's pinning
,cf.(of thousandes pluck*d*) unlucksome twins
Balan+Balin , & humbly scruple-siorfter *Bedwyn,*
aussi moroseate *Sanam of Guinntic,*
eke hight *Eglam* eke hight *Naram* et so many
autres et so many others;
moreover from over
th'ocean fleeting ships armorican
loyal *Cador* then'n'there commits; et
that f action of Gorre hold
ing *Lot's* cult abhored, head'd
by fiersome *Owain,* crafter-at-war
ne joind yet tacitsadly braced
Lot-m'other grievanced :*Rovæna*
fought awke-facèd family before, &
sad foredoomed, shall do once more

so s*if*ted out fromutuamidst **T**wain hosts
of hatredeath dealists all
woebegone w,ailing g'rind t'heir-teeth to s'word-edge
p'art for p'rep of carnage pat,*riot*'ic
where'pon whilst *Lot's* hosts o' disgr*un*tle

10 + w/in his command holding 489 cNights

stream chaunting de-parture

lô :::≈≈> un chartless t*Id*e groans

rolling Ynys Wydryn s'wells wyth faïrien waters rush its rimround
,echohush fog swathes surfs ascent alights
roundallabout moist air breathes murkysh light

& lô : : : : ≈≈> via haze reveiled still

eht *Ladie of Lakes* liketo melts
into mere-silt
calm-column ,as salt
-water creeps up-calves her
& she speaks:

***Ladie of Lakes*:** "well fa re , thee **B**oys –

i sea down stream p'our all thee
wretched woe & hetel sinnage stacked to Cloud , *as tides ,,*
& viathans of violances ere e'er , if e'er *,, ,asc,end her ' knees,*
untainted f'low ye quench in valric questage, *,,ripple,,*
and mickle a moon , ere e'er , if e'er
afresh we meet ; and moons a mickle *,,, , upslip ,, ,*
afore a,gain ye meet , as meet ye must,
young *arthur* ,: *anna* yr temnelpmoc twin; *, ,,her ' hippes;,, ,*
et either she to *th*wort or comfor't thee
: as per worthy's thine comport."

then outhaileth **arthur***:*

from his shrin,king shoure: "I *Ladie* **P**rithee : ,

sublim'nall –« *again* »– peep *, " ,,'w,'aves, " ,*
finale ap-point mentord tick *,, ' ,raised , ' , ~*
for maï-flush filial ever *,,' ,pas't her , '*
eyeball mine extr,action *~ , " w,aist ,, '*
absentwin my longlorn
hearthalf sister diastole?"

,” ,th,’s,well’ , ,,’
then laughter skips in dulcet s’tone *‘ ,lap’s her ac,olyte’s*
across th’in,creasing combers: *,,” ’ , should”ers ,;’ ~*

Ladie of Lakes: “pauvre **B**lind-th*k*ing*!* *’ , ;’ upc,rain’es her’ ,*

by id yr tenebrated sight *~ ,,” ,neck ’ , ,”upt,ilts ”*
saw not ! *arthur* , gr’son , hwæt: *’ , ,” ’; hera”colyte”sch,in’ ;,,*
yr si’ster si’lent magics *here* to-day *,;” ~’,”,,;swam,”p’til,, ” ’ ,*
pour *anna* tis mine acolyte,,,; *’,, ’ her acol,ytean’nas”~ , ,*
et sinkes now , at my besyde...” *’ , ’ ” , ’ ,;,, lip,s s’wim’,; , ’ , ”,, ’*
’ ~”—— into-th’foam...——,’ ~’

& when her **S**,poke-wordes die
th’inslets glass’s resmooth , unbroke.
...dumbstrick *arthurs* party roused
grimlyliche tourn about;
ceremonies’pin ,dry gears
g,et *Arthur* Wyrmwiht-c’rouwn’d
,C’loud-dis ,tracted sh,riven doubt –
;next oil s’words w/grease for tears
& muster up murder, pour Albions bliss.
straightaway=> *Ector* eht Council es*table*shes
round newle-king bout &
straightaway=> *Brastias* th’Warden of eht Sæxan Shoure
dubd, h’edges back Albions externenemies &
straightaway=> in-stalld’s th’Ste’ward *Bedwyn*
needling comptrollmatre &
straightaway=> ’tis *Caï* th’Seneschal named
h’ouer,seer of ovens &
Merlin , nary office nonhe takes
yet ever all ready hys
thority dif ,fused is.

thus : **C**losed

thys codex twinned immanentopia of ethrous *anna is*
,feyeryeic poeprophet
& frek *Arthur*
,ætheleste -~~king~~
's reign in blood born,e
ever to elderable sorrow,
tome of naîtrejoy by darkling chapters pieced&pincerd
ever as ever ô aye
;r*ecto*codex b'old-writ *Arthur* \||||/(whose *annA* versos palimpsest
& bloodshed rains dans => *volume pen-dyng*
pour Albion's muchel to learn
& Arthur's merit far a,part of Caliburn
& while *busilly* slaying armies sh'all burn
:tis *Anna's* turn.

Here Ends the First Volume of the Second Chronicle,
being the Sixth Book of *Arthur Dies.*

Appendix I:
Narrative Synopsis of the First Five Volumes
of the First Chronicle

Volume I

*two decades before arthur shall be born, the assembled hosts of the brythons assemble for the great funeral of **constantine**, pen-dragon of Albion, who has been slain by poison from an unknown hand. with constantine murdered by a treacherous unknown hand, his widow **Vivienne** guards with drawn knife her three young children: the youngest, **Uther**, passionate and impulsive; **Ambrosius-Merlinus**, of enigmatic mien; and cautious **Vortigern**, constantine's chosen heir. Uther crawls into the barrow's narrow passageway to see his dead father for the last time. there, he addresses several questions to the corpse, reflects upon the -king's reignand takes from the body caliburn, the legendary sword of Albion, ritually assuming the responsibility to become the arm of Albion, its will and force, to safeguard his people's capacity to act. Ambrosius-Merlinus enters his father's barrow after his brother has left it, questions the corpse, and takes from the body Albion's legendary shield, dargwthievoder, assuming responsibility to defend Albion from the onslaught of the World of the Real. in his turn, Vortigern, chosen by constantine as his heir, questions his dead father, ensnared in doubts. attempting to stroke his father's brow, he thrice flinches and thrice knocks the sacred armoured crown of Albion to the barrow's floor: a direful omen for his reign and for the people of Albion. overcome with horror, vortigern swoons, and lies unconscious, hidden in the shadows of the tomb. unaware that he remains, Vivienne enters and, after several questions, confides in him a secret: Merlinus-Ambrosius is no natural son of constantine, but the fruit of a night shared with one of the mirror-folk, those creatures of magic who act yet do not exist; out from her mirror, carved with magic characters, he had stepped and loved her. unknown to Vivienne, Vortigern has awoken and heard all. She withdraws, leaving vortigern alone, torn between love, duty, gratitude and ambition. at last he resolves to bury what he has heard, and say nothing of vivienne's secret.*

Volume II

*the year following constantine's death, **Vortigern** comes of age and takes the throne, but commands no respect. he shares his duties with his mother **Vivienne**, whose power has began to wane with her husband's demise. at the open council of Brythains, Vortigern's council debates, including **Blaise**, aged and reverend shaman just returned from the borderlands; **Maugantius**, wily advisor to many pen-dragons; and **Eldol**, a young and stalwart thane. grievous discord ensues.*

unsettled and swayed by the discourse of Maugantius, a slim majority of the brythons favour his proposal: ***Vortigern*** *will rule from a fixed centre, in hostile stance against the borderfolk, bolstered by the Sæx to ensure security with their blades. These measures enacted, their fortunes fare no better – all falls deeper into dire despair and decay, while evil omens flash across the land. Maugantius and his council therefore decree that Vortigern should build a mighty tower upon a tor in the 'kingdom's centre: for surveillance, co-ordination, and control. Albion's resources and labour are focused on this mighty venture, but to no avail: for each evening, the tower tumbles and sinks anew into the hungry earth.*

Maugantius gathers the Council of Albion to conduct an inquiry into the Towr's curse, with an array of ceremonial and magical investigations. finally, the Council as a whole oracles-forth by means of bibliomany, drawing sorts from potent books. as the Council of Lectors withdraws to debate the interpretation of the oracle, Vivienne asserts that the curse is that of Albion itself rejecting the coercive order of Rome, which the Towr seeks to re-erect. however, the majority of the Council, under the leadership of Maugantius, returns with the verdict that the curse is the result of a scandalous union between Mirrorman and Matre, and that union's offspring's blood must be strewn upon the Towr's foundations to secure them. Blaise and his acolyte ***Taliesin*** *deliver an outaged counter-interpretation, calling the majority reading the result of xenophobia, ethnic hate, and colonialism. they then carve a Sign of Dissent into their brows, declare their opposition to the emerging Fascist State, and depart from Ynys Wydryn.*

Vortigern meanwhile is struck dumb; for he knows a secret known to no other: Merlinus-Ambrosius was begotten on Vivienne by one of the Mirror-People. His conscience torn, Vortigern spends a night and a day wandering the moors, mad and ranting lamentations.

In the morn Vortigern publicly accuses Vivienne of consorting with the Mirror-Man, and orders that, according to the interpretation of the oracle, Merlinus-Ambrosius must be killed, and his blood scattered on the Towr's foundations to close the rift in reality and allow his stronghold to be completed.

Merlinus-Ambrosius is about to be killed when he begins to speak melodiously, in trance: from his words emerge a Prophesy of the Towr's fall and the regeneration of Albion. Maugantius convinces Vortigern that his prophesy represents treason, and the seer is sentenced to death. he is left imprisoned imprisoned in the pit beneath the Towr's foundations, to be executed the next day. in the night Vortigern and Maugantius come to try and entice or threaten him to support them, in order to save his own life; he refuses. they are still discoursing with him when Vivienne, having bloodily escaped the cell where she and Uther had been detained, appears and slices Maugantius' throat, slaying him and leaving Vortigern terrified and stunned. she, Uther, and Ambrosius-Merlinus erscape into the night.

Volume III

***Vivienne** having escaped with **Uther** and **Ambrosius-Merlinus** slain maugantius, now **Vortigern** surveys the carnage, finds himself friendless, fears for his security, and orders pursuit. revolt against his rule is brewing, led by the young thane **Eldol**. Vortigern orders the protests suppressed, but Albions army – voluntary and eternally provisional – resist his will. he retires to his Tor.*

*having escaped the City of Legions (formerly caerleon), the refugee pen-dragons skirt the coast, toward a hidden ship waiting to secrete them across the Sea of the Real to Armorica, land of Ban's people, of brythic kinship. first, they climb down a steep cliff overlooking the sea, in the midst of a great storm, where a concealed grotto is revealed to Vivienne. inside is the Crystal Cave, a dome of shattered mirrors, all reflected in a pool fed by a trickle of sea-water from above. it is a netherplace between Albion and the mirrorworld, and here a spell must be performed. inside, Ambrosius-Merlines stares at his broken, swaying reflection in the pool. Vivienne and her son weave a desperate spell: he is split in twain: his earthy self **Ambrosius** to flee to Armorica with her, his supernatural half **Merlinus** left in shamanic sleep in the mirrorworld.*

*the Pen-dragons escape across the Sea of the Real, aided and abetted by sympathetic brythons. Vortigern finds he has few friends remaining in Albion; paranoid, he withdraws from the public, disappearing into his now-completed fortress, and communicating only through brief, erratic notes dropped from the pinnacle of his towr. the fleet of Sæx and Ængals contracted by maugantius arrives on the coast. not trusting the free levies' loyalty to his person, he refuses to call up an army or organise defense. **Hængist** of the Sæx and **Hørsa** of the Ængals march unopposed through the City of Legions and present themselves to Vortigern with an ultimatum: he must honour maugantius' commitment to hire their arms in exchange for landed Property – a concept heretofore rejected by the brythons. desperate to support his regime, Vortigern agrees: the Ængals fight the State's external enemies under Hørsa and his son **Cerdic**; the Sæx police the brythons at home, reporting to **Hængist** at Vortigern's side. The spasm of civil unrest which results is speedily suppressed by the Sæx.*

*as agreed, Vortigern establishes the institution of Propety and grants it to the Sæx and Ængals. popular unrest is controlled as Hørsa's Ængals, fighting like mindless Drones, take the place of brythons in the borders, diminishing the latter's weight of guilt and trauma at the conflicts' horrors; as wealth from the wars benefits those willing to trade on foreign blood; and as the surveillance state established by Hængist's Sæx erodes the will to resistance and collaboration by spreading anxiety and distrust throughout society. nonetheless, many remain restive. the rogue shamans **Blaise** and **Taliesin** are still at large, fomenting revolt against the domination of Vortigern's Towr, evading the Sæx.*

*the resistance takes as its watchword **Arthur**, the mysterious vocable uttered by Ambrosius-Merlinus in prophetic trance when he predicted the Towr's fall. Vortigern then announces his betrothal to Hængist's daughter **Rovæna**, under unusual conditions: firstly because she is unitary and mortal, not a Matre born of Albion's collective will – secondly because the marriage is to be both permanent and monogamous, eschewing all potential bonds to place the –King solely in her orbit. Ire speads.*

relations are tense between the Sæx and Brythons attending the wedding ceremonies of Vortigern and Rovæna; the Sæx are armed, while most Brythons are not. at the feast, Hængist threatens any Brythons who attempt to contest the new regime, and offers the newlyweds a grisly gift: the captive rebel Eldol, whom he will torture and execute on the morrow.

Rovæna throws herself upon him and, speaking her own words for the first time, begs her husband and father to have mercy upon him; they relent, sparing his life but returning him to captivity. The Brythons doubt her sincerity, considering the whole affair to be political theatre. Alone that night, she reveals to Vortigern the secret history of the Sæx, and proposes that together they unite their peoples in sorority and turn away from Hængist's totalitarian path; though tempted, Vortigern refuses, affirming his trust in Hængist and the security state he is building.

the wars on the borders against the Gæls and Pictes continue, successfully prosecuted by Hørsa's Ængals; refugees stream into Albion, which is already wracked by famine. the Sæx, led by Hængist, solidify Vortigern's surveillance state, amassing reams of data on the citizens of Albion and infusing all with anxiety. meanwhile, the exiled pen-Dragons mature across the sea in Armorica, honing their skills in stewardship and combat, are slowly amassing an army to topple Vortigern's regime. Blaise and Taliesin remain at large, the former in communication with the pen-Dragons in Armorica.

then, Taliesin appears at the s'Tone Henge Henge, preaching passionately against the reign of Vortigern and Hængist. many of those inspired by his words and songs remain or return, their camp spreading across the fields around the dance of Giant sTones. with astonishing swiftness, and before the sæx can intervene, a provisional town has sprouted. there, an array of all those disaffected by the rule of the Towr form a myriad culture in defiance to that propagated by the regime, in which hundreds of matres, thanes and brythons form collectives, presses, cenacles, and bands, turning their sundry skills and passions to the continued evolution of Avalon's ways. they spread subversive songs, pictures, poems, masques, and tomes throughout Albion, in secret meeting-places, awaiting the pen-Dragons, and mysterious Arthur.

the Towr's council debates their inability to strike a mortal blow at this decentralized, always-changing network of dissent. Rovæna proposes a conciliatory meeting between the forces of Vortigern, his Sæx and Ængals, and

Taliesin's dissident phalanx centred at the Stone Circle, hoping to turn Vortigern away from Hængist's patriarchal, fascist policy; Hængist surprisingly agrees, and offers to release the Rebel Eldol there. the date set, cautious hope breathes again in Avalon.

four-hundred and fifty of ***Vortigern's*** *forces meet four-hundred and fifty citizens on the agreed day, both parties agreeing not to bear arms. after an initiatory ceremony, the conference begins with brief adresses by leaders on both sides; Hængist's true intention is unveiled. at his signal, the forces of the Towr draw the knives concealed in their boots and fall upon the un-armed citizens of Albion, slaughtering all except Eldol, who fights his way to safety and escapes, vowing vengeance. Rovæna attempts to stop the killing and is dragged from the field in chains, while the prisoner Taliesin is castrated, then returned to imprisonment and torture.*

Volume IV

Chapter 1

five years have passed since the massacre of Albion's folk at the s'Tone-Henge, upon the Night of the Long Knives. far removed from Albion, in the brythic enclave of Benoic, the exiled ***Pen-Dragons*** *– Vivienne, Ambrosius, and Uther – take shelter from the usurpers Vortigern and Hængist. Benoic's -king,* ***Ban****, is a supplemental spouse of* ***Vivienne****, now widowed of her primary husband, constantine.* ***Ambrosius****, now Vivienne's chosen heir, grows into a presciently wise and humble leader, just and dedicated, methodical and precise.* ***Uther****, even before passing childhood, proves himself a warrior worthy of legend in combat against Benoic's many foes, struggling for meagre resources. Gradually, Ban and the pen-Dragons gather refugees from both the Real and the tyranny of the Towr, amassing a phalanx – a mobile city on the bythons' traditional mould – which, when ready, shall first battle the fascists, then regrow Albion in peace and full humanity.*

Chapter 2

while the sæxan hegemony over Albion grows and the Ængals colonise the homes of the Pictes and Gæls, underground resistence continues, with Blaise and Eldol as motivating agents. They are in touch with the pen-Dragons in Benoic as they gradually prepare for their return, evading the spies of the Towr.

Chapter 3

*a vessel arrives at Ys, bearing a message from the pictish rebel **Uriens** to the exiled pen-Dragons. therein, he recounts the long tale of the Pictes' misfortunes, their colonisation by the Romans and then by the Brythons themselves. he reveals how **maugantius**, now dead, had fomented misery and dissent in the colonies, while hiding from Albion's people and Council the nature and extent of his actions. nonetheless, he now extends an offer of friendship and alliance against their common enemies in the Towr, on the basis of equality and justice.*

Chapter 4

*the Ængals are suspicious of **Rovæna's** sympathy for the Brythic prisoner **Taliesin**, and her father works with the Ængalic treason-hunter **Wlencing** to devise a test for her. before the assembled forces of the Towr and representatives of the Brythons, Taliesin (already castrated) is offered a bargain: he may go free on the condition that he sacrifice his tongue, swearing never again to speak against Vortigern's regime. when he refuses, Rovæna is asked to decide his sentence: should she grant him leniency, it will be proof of seditious leanings. spotting this trap, and after executing a strange dance of obscure significance, she proves her loyalty by demanding Taliesin's head. anon, Wlencing strikes the prophet's head from his body – but Lo! **Taliesin's Head** mounts into the air like a third orb of the sky, and utters a prophesy of the Towr's fall, the coming of the pen-Dragons, and the advent of* **Arthur**.

Chapter 5

*the Sæx and Ængals suspect, but cannot formulate or prove, Rovæna's complicity with Taliesin's last act of defiance, and the intelligence agenncies of both mercenary forces redouble their efforts to uncover the traitor in their midst. Wlencing seizes the brythic high priest **Guethenin,** Maugantius's successor and a puppet of the Sæx. under torture, Guethenin names **Rovæna** as the traitor, and the Ængals prepare a trap. warned, she flees the City of Legions north toward the Wall of Hadrian. on both sides of the Wall, a hybrid pictish-brythic culture is emerging, known as Gore or Gorre and led by **Uriens**. she joins Uriens and Blaise to nurture this counterculture against the Towr. Rovæna, revealing that her dance around Taliesin's body had been a ritual of divorce, announces a new wedding to her ally Uriens.*

Chapter 6

seven years after the pen-Dragons fled to refuge in Benoic, a dreadful prodigy in the form of a cyclopean dragon appears in the heavens over Albion, darkening the heavens in fearful apparition for many weeks, accompanied by draught and terror. in alignment the pen-Dragons launch their long-awaited expedition, with a mighty armada amassed by their Armorican allies, Ban and his son Riothamus. three phalanxes, fitted for war and for peace, set out, under the overall guidance of youthful Ambrosius. a storm of preturnatural fury arises suddenly from the calm Sea, and the fleet is whisked far from their prepared course – and away from the eyes of the Towr's spies. they emerge miraculously unharmed at Totnes, dispersing the startled and unprepared garrison and freeing the town, which demolishes the new stone buildings and reverts to a nomadic phalanx, supplied by Vivienne's steward-army with pavilions. the next morning, the portent in the sky vanishes, and the westcountry rises in rebellion against the Towr. the pen-Dragons are joined by war-troupes led by **Ygraine** *of Cornwall, with her consort* **Gorlois**. *Together they liberate Exeter, and prepare to face the Towr's gathering forces.*

Chapter 7

News of the pen'Dragon's landing and their capture of Exeter arrives at the Towr, prompting infighting between the Ængals and the Sæx. **Hængist** *makes plans both with and apart from* **Hørsa**, *and makes a futile visit to* **Vortigern**, *with whom communication is impossible since Rovæna's defection to the cause of Albion.*

Chapter 8

In a ruse planned by Ambrosius, the pen-Dragons split their forces on either side of the river Severn as they move north toward the Towr, drawing the Sæx into battle at Mæsbeli. Their fortunes fluctuate in the battle's first stages. At last with the combined efforts of Uther's valour, the support of Ygraine's & Eldol's revolutionary tribes, **Riothamus**' *fleet, and battle-engines designed by Ambrosius, the brython alliance defeats the Sæx, and Eldol slays Hængist in the field.* **Octa**, *judging the battle impossible to win, ignores Hængist's call for aid and abandons his army, instead collecting the refugees to salvage the power of the Sæx and fight another day.*

Chapter 9

as the pen-Dragons close in on Towr in the City of Legions, the Ængals under Hørsa recall their troops from the colonies to defend it, while Octa's Sæx successfully suppress uprisings and recover from their defeat at Mæsbeli. meanwhile Uriens and Rovænna allied launch a revolt of united Pictes and Brythons, declaring the new rePublic of Gore, ambushing and killing the army of the hated ***Wippid****. Ambrosius and Uther surround the garrison of the City and Towr, composed of the new brythic client-kings working for the Sæx; but Hørsa, joined by* ***Eøbessa****, then surrounds them in turn, trapping them between two hostile armies. the phalanx of Totnes remains free, planting crops and spreading culture until attacked by an Ængalo- Sæxan force led by the feared* ***Cerdic****, returned from Gæland, who massacres over 7000 and kills Ban and nearly* ***Vivienne*** *before their rescue by Riothamus' fleet.*

Chapter 10

the pen-Dragon army is trapped between the besieged Sæxan garrison of the City of Legions, and the Ængalish army encircling it in turn. hoping to crush it and reap the spoils alone before the arrival of Octa's fresh Sæxan force, Hørsa's Ængals attack the pen-Dragons' outer ring, defended by Uther. the armies strive viciously, and in the combat Eldol slays Eøbessa, Hørsa's younger son. Uther faces Hørsa in single combat is set to slay him, when he sees Ygraine wounded, dragging her consort Gorlois to safety. straightaway he leaves Hørsa alive in his rush to rescue her; he leaves her bleeding wife on the field, to be saved by Eldol's warband. as evening advances, Octa's Sæxan army appears and advances to join the Ængals; but they are met by a light brythic force of warships and archers on their flank by the Severn river, and fighting halts for the night.

Chapter 11

The Towr is set aflame as the phalanx is liberated by the pen-Dragon forces, and Vortigern, trapped alone inside with his mnemnomancers, burns to death.

Chapter 12

the people of Albion celebrate their liberation and topple the stone buildings, monuments, and institutions of Vortigern's totalitarian regime – freeing the mobile phalanx of Cærleon from the fetters of the sedantary "City of Legions". the remaining bands of Sæxan police and Ængalic troops unleash violence on the citizens, but are overcome. the allies diffuse throughout Albion and Armorica, spreading a rebirth through mutual aid, coordination, and diversity, though hostile ængalsæx remain in Gælish colonies and the Sæxan Shore, combatted by Uther. on Alban Arthuan, the Solstice, Vivienne conducts her own funeral rites in the city of Ys, dies, and is reborn as the Lady of Lakes. (The Cloud persists.)

Chapter 13

the people of renewed Albion gather at Stonehenge to commemorate those murdered there by the Sæx and Ængals in the Night of the Long Knives. Pictes, Gæls, those among the Ængals and Sæx who have renounced domination and exploitation, and the new multicultural community of Gorre all join the ceremony as equal citizens of Albion, despite some brythons' objections. after drinking from the fourth ritual cup, Ambrosius' discourse grows loose, errant, disintegrant; he grows ashen, flickers, weakens; his mnemnomancers fall suddenly into madness: he has been poisoned! in the chaos, some among the crowd revert to Sæx-induced habits and immediately accuse the Pictes and other minority peoples, and threaten those present; when Uther is too distraught over his brother's death to take note, Eldol steps in to prevent violence. suddenly, a strange figure appears, throbbing with magic and donning a plague mask: - Merlinus, Ambrosius' mirror-half, returned from long hibernation to call Arthur into the World.

Volume V

Chapter 1

as the mourning ***Uther*** *takes the reins from the slain ambrosius, Albion is invigorated by the first blossomings of an equitable society – yet also beset by renewed sæxan and ængalic assaults, plague, and famine caused by The Cloud left from the Towr's destruction, and the robber-Barons who still exploit many brythons in the name of Property, added to the instability of the assassination's aftermath. advised closely by his br'other, the mysterious young magus -* ***Merlinus****, Uther sees personally to defense as* ***Eldol*** *sees to the legal arrest and sentence of the assassin, and morg****Ygraine*** *and* ***Gorlois*** *make nurturemancy continue to flourish.* ***Uriens*** *and* ***Rovæna****, who have conceived and birthed their heir* ***Lot****, force the last colonists out of the new Republic of Gorre, and begin* *to demolish the Wall of the Romans; but the ousted colonists join the force of barons, sæx, and ængals amassing under the leadership of the baron* ***Pascentricius*** *on the coast for an invasion of Gæland.*

Chapter 2

the invasion of **Pascentricius** *is initially successful as some of the former ængalic colonies are reoccupied by his barons. the gælish resistance coalesces around the young -king* ***Gilloman****, who scores an early victory followed by a stinging defeat. on the advice of the bard* ***Fedelme*** *he sends the latter to beg aid from* ***Uther*** *and the brythons, whose wars have prompted the invasion. for aid in the form of food, supplies, and weapons Gilloman offers lasting alliance; but should Uther come himself with battle-phalanxes, Gilloman promises a greater gift: the enchanted standing stones of the Giants' Dance at Killaire. Uther agrees and comes to Gæland, where he joins Gilloman's force and smashes that of* Pascentricius. *in the games and feasting after the victory, neither the bands of the gæls nor those of the brythons can bring down the standing stones, but goaded by Fedelme,* ***Merlinus*** *does so with a machine of magic and bears them back to be added to Amesbury's Stone Henge, a memorial to his otherself ambrosius and those slain in the Night of the Long Knives.*

Chapter 3

after re-raising the Giants Dance at te Stone Henge at Amesbury, ***Merlinus*** *informs* ***Uther*** *that he is leaving to seek the magus Blaise and offer himself as apprentice, much to the dismay of Uther, who depends greatly on his council. upon parting, Merlinus warns Uther that the prophesy of Arthur is not inevitable, gravely urging patience and self-restraint. Uther winters in Cærleon, where his attentions to morg****Ygraine****, first consort of* ***Gorlois****, become pronounced. Ygraine refuses to desert or demote her primary consort, though Uther may not form a secondary union until after Arthur's generation, nor may she bear Arthur as a third-child, lest his generation be go astray: thus Uther and Ygraine must wait to fulfill their desire. when the couple depart for Cærnwellen, the -king is seized by an insanity of lust and rage, declaring a rebellion. he loses the support of* **Eldol** *and* **Riothamus** *and many among the brythons who fear incipient tyranny; but his page* ***Ulfin*** *offers to entice Merlinus to return and use magic to win Ygraine, & goes to seek him.*

Chapter 4

*charged by **Uther,** his page **Ulfius** seeks to find **Merlinus** & beg his aid to consummate his infatuation with **morgYgraine**. Merlinus gives him a formula capable of temporarily dissolving the barriers between the identities of thanes and matres, after Ulfius deceives him into believing that all parties involved wished for the same cosummation, thus to avoid war; the magus then continues on his way. Meanwhile, Uther's armies are besieging the forces led by **Gorlois** in the Cast,le Terrible and those led by Ygraine in the Cast'le Tintagel. Uther activates the magical formula, stealing Gorlois' Form and, unknown to him, rendering her comatose. In her form, Uther joins his thoughtseed with Ygraine, conceiving Arthur. Yet at the last moment, half-realising that her ~~lover's~~ true identity, she sacrifices much of her life-force to manifest Arthur fully despite her own depleted forces. The result is the seed of a double-child, a set of twin pen-Dragons: **Arthur** and his selfsister **Anna**. In the meantime, Ulfius uses the formula himself to sneak unrecognised into the Cast'le Terrible, where in order to protect the new heir's legitimacy, he murders Gorlois as she sleeps.*

Chapter 5

*aghast and outraged at **Uther's** betrayal, **Ygraine** curses him, declaring that Arthur and Anna shall not leave her womb until their father lies dead. Uther offers certain apologies, which are not accepted. **Merlinus** is likewise castigated by Ygraine for his role, and goes mad from guilt. meanwhile Uther is called to the Sæxan Shore to repel a new invasion by the Sæx & Ængals.*

Chapter 6

*in his madness **merlinus** flees to the Forest Perilous, lamenting his guilt and wreaking destruction until he meets the **Questing Beast.** after three months in the Forest, he is discovered by **Brastius**, sent by Ygraine to find him. subdued by Brastias' sympathetic music, merlinus returns and meets **Ygraine** and her children **Mark** and **Ause**, prophesying on each; but upon reaching Tintagel, he is appalled by the crowds of people and his madness returns. he flees again into the Forst Perilous, living like a beast of the woods. autumn, then winter assail him mercilessly, until he wanders into the camp of his brother's army. there **Uther**, terminally ill, proposes that they heal each other, and builds a golden cage to contain merlin's madness; but merlin states that there is no undoing Ygraine's curse. Uther releases him, and he journeys on a ship of fools to Gæland, where the bard-que'en **Fidelme** befriends and cares for him as an autre ~~sister~~. at last his madness passes, & he returns on the eve of AnnArthurs' impending birth.*

Chapter 7

dying of Ygraine's curse and shorn of allies, bedridden ***Uther's*** *leadership falters. after Gorre repulses an ængalic invasion,* ***Hørsa & Octa*** *both attack the brythons, & the fortunes of war swing forth and back.* ***Merlin****, his madness now controlled, arrives & builds for the dying -king a fearsome battle-litter to carry Uther into combat, from which he can fight Albion's enemies even on his death-bed. he rides into the fight upon this chariot-cot, wreaking great violence on the enemy. At last he slays first Octa, then Hørsa, spiking their heads upon his bedposts as the sæxængalic shield-walls collapse & the victory falls to to Albion.*

Chapter 8

Ygraine *goes into childbirth at the same moment as* ***Uther*** *is joining combat on the opposite side of Albion; bound by her curse that Uther would die before his children are born, and too weak through previous emanations to bear the pen-Dragon twins, her labour lasts for a full week.* ***Merlin*** *brings the dying Uther to Tintagel in his death-carriage, where he officially bequeaths his duties to the impending first-born, then dies. Ygraine gives birth first to* ***Arthur****, then to* ***Anna*** *– but in doing so she gives her own life. before she dies, Ygraine sends* ***Arthur*** *with* ***Brastias*** *to be raised in secret by the thane* ***Ector****, and* ***Anna*** *to be hidden in Ys along with Caliburn, s'word of Albion's strength. Merlin, refusing the succession, appoints as Arthur's regent over Albion* ***Eldol****, who weds* ***Riothamus*** *and restores the alliance with Benoic, producing two children; yet the Sæxan Shoure still poses threats, spurred by a new monotheistic cult among the Ængals, and the armed Barons still ply exploitation, and there are mutterings within the regency. Merlin returns and calls a great gathering at the Stone Henge, where he drives an enchanted S'word through an anvil into a S'tone, revealing that the one who can draw the S'word out again shall be Arthur, prepared to claim his duties.*

Appendix II:

Dramatis Personæ

of Principal Characters

*Each character's trajectory is given from Volume I through the end of the present volume, inclusive. A character's actions in each volume are indicated by Chronicle number in roman numerals and volume in arabic numerals, thus: **I,2** = Chronicle I, Volume 2. Characters with their own entries are marked by italics.*

Ægwissance: A sæxan priestess to Yaldabaoth, the monotheistic deity brought by *Colgrimliche*. ***II,1*** – She brought her congregation to the great tournament at the s'Tone Henge in the hopes that, by drawing the s'Word from the s'Tone, she could secure her authority, prove the ascendency of Yaldabaoth, and rule in his name as arthur. When she failed to draw the s'Word, she joined the Gorrish opposition to *Arthur* in a bid to salvage her damaged status, accusing him and his supporters of charlatanry, and eventually joined *Lot's* forces for the war against Arthur.

Anna: Twin and self-sister of *Arthur*, daughter of *Ygraine* & *Uther,* half-sister of *Ause* & *Mark*. ***I,5*** – Arthur was the pen-Dragon long prophesied for Albion; Anna was the pen-Dragon long prepared in silence, un-knowing, in the prophesy's shadow. Her becoming was sparked when Ygraine, at the moment of Arthur's conception, realised Uther's deception and violation; Ygraine withheld some part of herself from Arthur's seed, refusing the violence of Uther's inheritance, dividing and diverting the surge of generation, and in the space of this withdrawal the seed of Anna was planted. As he died, Uther bequeathed his own duties on whichever child would be first-born; this lot fell to Arthur. To Anna fell the duties to aid and encourage him in his establishment of harmony, to restrain and oppose him in his weilding of power. On her mother's dying orders, Anna was taken by *Brastias* to Ys, in Benoic, to be raised by a certain Lady he would meet in there. ***II,1*** – Anna's whereabouts long remained unknown, though rumour had her visiting, in her childhood, the Lady of Lakes in the cavern-waters underneath Ys. In the months leading up to her twin's investiture as pen-Dragon she surreptitiously appeared as one of the lake-ladies to several people in several places, but was not truly revealed until Arthur's investiture at Ynys Wydryn, where she accompanied the *Lady of Lakes* as an acolyte, her identity secret and her presence unnoticed until the final seconds of her visit, when her identity was unveiled at last.

AnnArthur: The embryonic dyad which, when born, was manifest as Anna and Arthur.

Arthur: The pen-Dragon long prophesied to generate Albion's renewal; son of *Ygraine* and *Uther*, twin and self-brother of *Anna*. First invoked by *Merlinus-Ambrosius* in his prophetic trance at the foot of the Tow*r* in ***I,2***. A talisman, magical vocable, a victorious cry from an uncertain future; a prophesy in the process of articulation; an evocation of hope and love; a future pen-Dragon in the womb of Albion's ludic desires. A watchword, a curse on the Real, pen-Dragon in imminence. ***I,5*** – Arthur was conceived in Tintagel, in an act of violation and deceit, a product of self-deluded lust. Within him the strains of the ideal were crossed those of lust, strains of love with those of power; his twin sister Anna was constituted to aid and encourage him in the establishment of harmony, to restrain and oppose him in the weilding of power. As he died, Uther bequeathed his duties on whichever child would be first-born; this lot fell to Arthur. On his mother's dying orders, Arthur was taken by *Brastias* to the thane *Ector*, who would raise him in secrecy, unaware of his parentage. Merlin then called a great gathering at the Stone Henge, where he drove an enchanted S'word through an anvil into a S'tone, revealing that the one who could draw the S'word out again would be Arthur, prepared to claim his duties. ***II,1*** – Knowing nothing of his origins, the young thane was called Wortimer, or Wort, until the drawing of the s'Word from the s'Tone. He was squire to his older foster-brother *Caï,* a young Gastromancer, and accompanied him and Ector to the great Tournament at the s'Tone Henge, where Caï would compete in the cooking contests. Having lost Caï's b*read*knife at a musical contest at which the pair had stopped to dance earlier during the tournament, Wortimer/Arthur left Caï at the lists awaiting his turn to compete, as Arthur returned to seek the knife. Not finding it, he dimly recalled the s'Word at the s'Tone Henge, but not its significance. Determined to find a blade for Caï, he attempted thrice to pull the s'Word from the s'Tone, succeeding on the final attempt. From this moment, the seedling consciousness of Arthur began dissolving that of Wort in the process of transformation. When Ector and Caï recognised the s'Word, a contest was held at the s'Tone Henge, where Arthur alone could draw it. Those present were divided, and a new contest was set for the Winter Solstice. The results were the same, and a third contest set for the next Mayday, where Wort once again drew the s'Word, and his investiture ceremony was set for Lammas. He came to this ceremonial festival in high spirits, though surrounded by a watchful bodyguard. During the traditional period of the King-as-Fool, *Lot* exploited the licence granted by the rite to assail Arthur, first in mocking terms but then in deadly earnest, finally declaring that they would not take part in his investiture, nor recognise his lead, resulting at last in the splitting of Albion as each side prepared for civil war. Meanwhile the *Lady of Lakes* reminded all assembled there that the s'Word in the s'Tone granted, at most, a provisional legitimacy, revealing that the true s'word of the pen-Dragons, Caliburn, was in her keeping and would only be given to one who had earned it. As the Lady, remaining neutral, departed under the rising tide, Arthur begged her to divulge the whereabouts of his twin, whereupon she revealed that her acolyte, at that moment being swept away by the sea, was in fact Anna – too late for them to speak on this occasion. Arthur proceeded to appoint his provisional government, and to prepare for war.

Ause: Matre-child of Cærnwellen, daughter of *Ygraine & Gorlois*, sister to *Mark* and half-sister to *Anna & Arthur*. ***I,5*** – Still an infant, Ause and her brother were taken by his mother to meet *Merlin* during his madness, where the seer prophesied great power in the child's future. ***II,1*** – After Ygraine's death, Ause was fostered by her loyal page *Brastias*, who served as regent.

[illegible]

Balan: Twin brother of *Balin*. ***II,1*** – The youthful Balan and Balin had little interest in politics, but attended the Tournament at the s'Tone Henge primarily to participate in its spectacle and excitement. Balan attempted on a whim to draw the s'Word at the second contest and was little concerned at his failure. He was among *Arthur's* first supporters, and quickly established himself as a formidable warrior.

Balin: Twin sister of *Balan*. ***II,1*** – The youthful Balan and Balin had little interest in politics, but attended the Tournament at the s'Tone Henge primarily to participate in its spectacle and excitement. Balin attempted on a whim to draw the s'Word and was little concerned at her failure. She was among *Arthur's* first supporters, and quickly established herself as a formidable warrior.

Bedwyn: a Matre known for their sense of disinterested duty. ***II,1*** – During the tournament at the s'Tone Henge, Bedwyn was the first outside *Wortimer's* family to notice that the s'Word had been drawn from the s'Tone, and raised the general hue and cry, and soon became one of Wortimer/Arthur's first supporters, supporting his claim against the boy's many opponents and volunteering for his bodyguard at the investiture on Lamas, and finally being appointed Arthur's steward, managing the daily operations of his administration.

Blaise: Elder Shaman of Avalon and ally of the pen-Dragons, leader of intellectual resistance to the hegemony of the *Tower* in the days of Arthur's forebears; mentor of *Taliesin*. ***I,2*** – Blaise spent many years among the Pictes and Gaels, and claimed that they were brethren of Albion and the warfare against them was illegitimate. He opposed the establishment of Vortigern's *Tower*; together with Taliesin, he dissented against the augury to sacrifice *Ambrosius-Merlinus*. They evaded the *Tower's* spies while circulating Albion, spreading sedition around the watchword ARTHUR. ***I,3*** – Blaise traveled secretly overseas to join the pen-Dragons in exile, coordinating the resistance with Taliesin's network in Albion and teaching young Ambrosius. ***I,4*** – Blaise became the pen-Dragons' intermediary with *Uriens* and *Rowena*. ***I,5*** – Once the Tower had fallen and Albion seemed to be secure in *Uther's* stewardship, *Merlin* sought out Blaise and retired from public service for a time to serve as his apprentice until Blaise's death.

Brastias: Musician and loyal page of *Gorlois,* later a leader among the Cærnish. ***I,5*** – When *Ulfin* determined to assassinate Gorlois, he used the portion of *Merlinus*' formula to take the trusted Brastias' form, thereby gaining access to Terrible Castle to carry out his deed. After the first phase of Merlin's madness, *Ygraine*, taking pity on him, sent Brastias to lure the magician back to society by means of his enchanting music. Brastias, taking his lyre into the Forest Perilous, succeeding in doing so, though the effect proved temporary. In the Spring, he was sent to command the Cærnish war-phalanx as part of *Uther's* army, despite his bitterness toward the -king for Ygraine's violation and Gorlois' murder. Arriving as *Eldol's* forces were being pushed back, Brastias helped to turn the tide of the campaign and push the Ængals back until the arrival of fresh forces under *Colgrimliche*. After Merlin constructed Uther's battle-litter, Brastias' phalanx was appointed as the -king's bodyguard. With her dying breath, Ygraine sent Brastias in secrecy to deliver Arthur to be raised with *Ector*, and *Anna* to the *Lady of Lakes* in the city of Ys – after taking from Uther's corpse Caliburn, the s'word of Albion, to leave with the Lady. **II,1** – After Ygraine's death, Brastias fostered Ygraine's & Gorlois' children *Mark* and *Ause*, serving as their regent, keeping hidden from all the secret of Anna's whereabouts. They traveled to the s'Tone Henge for the great Tournament, where Brastias was initially skeptical about *Wort*'s identity as

Arthur, but after attempting to pull the s'Word himself and then watching Wort, Brastias became one of the first converts to his cause. At the second trial, he accused Arthur's opponents of repeating the betrayal of Cærnwellen first perpetrated by Uther a generation later, by refusing the legitimacy of the heir he created through that betrayal. He volunteered for Arthur's bodyguard at the investiture on Lammas, where the Lady of Lakes finally revealed Anna, relieving Brastias of his secret. Following Arthur's investiture, he was named Warden of the Sæxon Shoure.

Cabal: The hound of the young *Arthur*/Wortimer. ***II,1*** – Cabal was the only mortal witness to Wort-Arthur's initial drawing of the s'Word from the s'Tone. The dog did not care a whit.

Cador: Scion of Armorica, infant son of *Riothamus* and *Eldol*, twin brother of *Budicca*. ***I,5*** - Buddica and Cador were born in the year between the birth of *Anna* & *Arthur* and the planting of the S'word in the s'tone. ***II,1*** – Cador was brought by Eldol to the second trial of the s'Word in the s'Tone, where he tried and failed to draw the s'Word despite being even younger than *Wortimer/Arthur*, whose cause he vocally supported in the ensuing debates. At the third trial of the s'Word and the s'Tone, Cador made the most strident claim on Arthur's behalf and rallied support to him, later volunteering for his bodyguard at the investiture on Lamas. There, when *Lot* insulted Arthur and denied the legitimacy of his leadership, Cador grew enraged and called upon the *Lady of Lakes* to support Arthur's claim – a request that she rebuked, considering their dispute petty. Instead she reminded them all that the s'Word in the s'Tone was not Caliburn, s'Word of the pen-Dragons, but merely the war-s'word of dead *Uther*, making its wielder merely duc of battles. Cador immediately promised an alliance between Armorican and Arthur, and pledged the Armorican armada in his support in the civil war.

Caï: Son of *Ector*, Foster-Brother of *Wortimer/Arthur*. ***II,1*** – Caï apprenticed as a Gastromancer, and upon coming into his own, went to compete in the cooking contests at the great Tournament at the s'Tone Henge, accompanied by his father and his foster-brother, serving as his squire. Having lost his b*read*knife at a musical contest at which the pair had stopped to dance earlier during the tournament, *Wortimer*/Arthur left Caï at the lists awaiting his turn to compete, as Wortimer went to seek the knife. On Wort's return, Caï upbraided him, not recognising the s'Word. Seeing Ector upset upon seeing it, Caï believed Wort was in trouble, and twice took the blame for stealing the s'Word twice; when he realized the blade's identity, he admitted that it was Arthur who had drawn it. Along with other contestants that day, Caï attempted and failed to draw the s'Word himself later that day, and despite his sadness over Wort's dissolution into Arthur, became one the -king's first supporters and volunteered for his bodyguard at the investiture at Ynys Wydryn, later being appointed his seneschal and placed in charge of the hospitality of Arthur's cenacle.

Carados: Leader of a gorrish phalanx. ***II,1*** – Carados supported *Lot* as the potential Arthur prior to the drawing of the s'Word from the s'Tone. One of Lot's most fanatical followers, he was prone to spinning conspiracy theories against his competitors, and joined his phalanx to the forces of Lot against *Arthur*.

Caudebennett: Baron based in the region Bernicia, known as the "No-Bo[d]y of Bernicia". ***II,1*** – Caudebennett and his band attended the tournament where *Wortimer/Arthur* drew the s'Word from the s'Tone. When Caudebennett failed to draw it in the contest there, he joined opposition to Wortimer/Arthur, arguing that he was too weak and untried to control Albion, later joining the Corporation of Barons against Arthur.

Cerdic: Warlord of the Ængals, brother of *Eøbessa*, son of *Hørsa* son of Aelle. ***I,3*** – Directed military operations against the Gæls to the west, eventually invading the mainland of Æire. Subject of many hostile gælish and brythic folk-ballads. ***I,4*** – Returning to the main island in the campaign against the pen-Dragons, he employed the same tactics against the revolting brythons, attacking *Vivienne's* peacephalanx with chemical weapons adapted from those devised by *Ambrosius*, and massacring 7000, including *Ban* of Benoic. ***II,1*** – One of the few Ængalic leaders of his generation to survive the defeat of the Towr, over the following decade Cerdic gradually rose to tenuous control of the Ængalo-Sæxan confederation.

Clariance: A matre leading an albrithionic cenacle focused on the mechanical arts. ***II,1*** – present at the Festival of the s'Word in the s'Tone at the Henge, she attempted to draw the s'Word herself in the final trial using ingenious machines, yet failed, later joining the army against *Arthur*.

Colgrimliche: Ængalish monotheistic warrior-priest. ***I,5*** – Colgrimliche led a mercenary war-band called in by *Hørsa*, who arrived at the perfect moment to halt the advance of Albion's armies under Eldol and save the hard-pressed Hørsa. His monotheistic cult quickly spread among the Ængals along the Saexan Shoure after the deaths of Hørsa and *Octa*. ***II,1*** – By the time of Arthur's return, the cult of Yaldabaoth, led by Colgrimliche, had become a major political force throughout the Sæxan Shoure, and was even making inroads among the brythons.

Crandallmas: A middling baron converted to the cult of *Lot*, whose bands defrauded folk through bureaucratic rather than physical means. ***II,1*** – Baron Crandalmas argued at the council following the second trial of the s'Word&s'Tone that the miracle should be discounted, and Albion submitted to a consistent, controlling power that would prevent all discord and deviance – either a technocratic bureaucracy or a military regine. An early convert to the cult of Lot, he was among the first to join the forces opposing *Arthur* after failing to draw the s'Word himself in the final trial.

Cutha: A minor priest of Yaldabaoth stationed in the Crow's Leah colony on the frontier of the Sæxan Shoure. ***II,1*** – Cutha was reportedly the first to behold *Anna*, in the person of the lady of a lake. He went mad, last seen wandering in the Forest Perilous.

Dubryc: Chief Hierophant of Albion at the time of *Arthur's* return, successor of *Gratianus*. ***II,1*** - When the great Dragon appeared for the second time in the sky above Albion, Dubryc joined *Eldol* in calling for a great council at the Stone Henge, whereat any may attempt to draw the S'word from the S'tone, though none had succeeded before. When *Wortimer/Arthur* unexpectedly drew the s'Word, Dubryc oversaw the resulting contest, and later Arthur's investiture as duc of battles and provisional pen-Dragon.

Ector: Obscure but stalwart thane, father of *Caï*, and *Arthur's* foster-father. ***I,5*** – With her dying breath, *Ygraine* sent *Brastias* in secrecy to deliver Arthur, under the name of Wortimer, to be raised with Ector in secrecy, lest he be killed or corrupted in his innocence. Ector knew not the origin of the child, but could not help but suspect. ***II,1*** – Both suspecting yet doubting "Wortimer's" potential to be Arthur, Ector brought his born-son Caï and Wortimer to the Tournament at the s'Tone Henge. After Wortimer/Arthur drew the s'Word from the s'Tone Ector, though grieving at the impending dissolution of Wort's identity in Arthur's, was one of his initial supporters, overseeing his bodyguard at the investiture at Ynys Wydryn and helping to organise a council of experienced elders to advise him in the struggle against the armies of *Lot* and the barons.

Eglam: A bellicose thane. ***II,1*** – Eglam attempted and failed to draw the s'Word from the s'Tone on the final attempt. Eglam's phalanx supported *Arthur* in the civil war against *Lot* and the barons.

Eldol: Influential thane, leader of political resistance to the hegemony of the Tow*w*r, loyal ally of the pen-Dragons. ***I,2*** – Eldol first achieved recognition as a young thane who challenged *Vortigern's* coup d'etat, his resistance ended only by a dozen spear-tips. Gathering other dissidents, he rescued the pen-Dragons and made arrangements for their safe transport to *Ban* in Armorica. ***1,3*** – Eldol became the most outspoken activist against Vortigern's regime, soon forced into hiding. After the arrival of the Sæx, he was tracked down, captured, and tortured by *Hængist*. In the Night of the Long Knives, his life was saved by Rovæna, slew sixty of the Tow*w*r's soldiers, and became the only survivor of the massacre. ***I,4*** – As a refugee, Eldol gathered a guerrilla force which struck by cultural and martial means against the occupiers. He joined the pen-Dragon army in an amphibious landing at the battle of Mæsbeli where he slew Hængist in combat to avenge his torture. At the memorial ceremony for the Night of the Long Knives, of which he was the only survivor, he stepped forward to prevent ethnic violence in the immediate wake of Ambrosius' assassination. ***I,5*** – Eldol was placed in charge of the border with the Sæxan Shoure, repelling and launching raids along it. When Uther declared Cærnwellen in rebellion, he objected and was the first thane to openly refuse participation in the campaign. Nonetheless, when the Ængalo-Sæxan invasion was launched, as Uther languished in his sick-bed, Eldol led the armies in the field against *Octa's* Sæx. He fought in Uther's final battle, and was later appointed regent of Avalon until Arthur's return. In the first year of his regency, Eldol wed *Riothamus*, repairing the rift between Albion and Armorica created by Uther. ***II,1*** – Merlin served as Albion's regent for three years before passing the role to *Eldol*, to hold until Arthur's reappearance. When the great Dragon appeared for the second time in the sky above Albion, Eldol joined *Dubryc* in calling for a great council at the Stone Henge, whereat any may attempt to draw the S'word from the S'tone, though none had succeeded before. After Wortimer/Arthur drew the s'Word, Eldol faced strong opposition from Gorre and the Barons if he immediately recognised him as Arthur; therefore, after consulting with Merlin, he called for a second contest at the Winter Solstice. The same occurred at the Solstice, with a third contest on May-Day. When Arthur remained alone in drawing the s'Word, Eldol and Merlin overruled the opposition of Lot and the Barons to set his installation ceremony at Ynys Wydryn. Relieved of his duties as regent after Arthur's investiture, Eldol led Albion's old guard, those who had served under Uther, to rally to his cause and served as a close military advisor.

Fedelme: Bard and later Que'en of the Gæls, consort of *Gilloman*, mother of *Gurman*. ***I,5*** – During the invasion of Gæland by the colonial brythic barons under *Pascentricius*, Fidelme as bard and spiritual leader proposed an alliance with Albion, and gained it with *Merlin's* support. At the celebration after the joint armies' victory, she challenged Merlin to topple a stone from the Giants' Dance at Killaire, which he achieved. She wed the -king *Gilloman*, fathering *Gurmun*, father in turn of Yseult and Morold. In the following year, Merlin returned to Gæland on a ship of fools, and was found naked and starving in the forest by Fedelme, who cared for him as an autre-~~sister~~, gradually nursing him back to health and guiding him as he finally passed through his madness. ***II,1*** – Wary of involvement in the wars of Albion, Fidelme and Gilloman kept Gæland neutral in the struggles over Arthur's ascension.

Gilloman o Niall: -king of the Gæls of Leinster, consort of *Fedelme*, father of *Gurman*. **I,5** – Gilloman was crowned on the very day of the invasion by*Pascentricius*' and his barons, yet it was he who initiated the first successful gælish response and became the rallying-point of resistance. On the advice of the bard *Fedelme*, he applied to *Uther* for help driving the colonists out. He led the federated warbands of the Gæls into battle alongside Uther, and killed *Pascentricius* in the fighting. He wed the bard Fedelme, fathering *Gurmun*, father in turn of Yseult and Morold. ***II,1*** – Wary of involvement in the wars of Albion, Fidelme and Gilloman kept Gæland neutral in the struggles over Arthur's ascension.

Gorlois: [illegible] consort of Ygraine, [illegible] of Carnwellion, mother of [illegible]. *I,4* – She nonetheless accompanied Ygraine on the campaign of liberation against the Saxons and [illegible] independent pledges of arms and peace [illegible], then fought alongside Ygraine at the Battle of the Tome. *I,5* – After the fall of Tome, Gorlois joined Ygraine with the [illegible], [illegible] the west-country [illegible]. *Uther's* attraction to Ygraine grew, until Gorlois prevailed upon Ygraine to return with her to Carnwellion. Uther, enraged, pressed Ygraine to renounce her. When she refused, the s-King declared Carnwellion in rebellion and called Albion to arms against it. Splitting their forces between two impregnable hill-forts, Ygraine was fortified at the Castle Tintagel, while Gorlois held its sister fort, the Castle Terrible; both were besieged by Uther's forces. When Uther used Merlins' identity-dissolving formula to assume Gorlois form and deceived Ygraine in order to conceive Arthur, Gorlois herself was thrown into an existential coma, her element unfixed to her form. While she was thus incapacitated, and while Uther lay with her wife in Tintagel, his crony *Ulfin* snuck into Castle Terrible without orders and, in order to protect the future Arthur's birthright, murdered her in her bed.

Guenefaire: Daughter of *Leodegrance*. ***II,1*** – The young Guenefaire accompanied her father to the great tournament at the s'Tone Henge where Wortimer-*Arthur* first drew the s'Word from the s'Tone.

Gurman: Child of -king *Gilloman* and queen *Fedelme* of Gæland/[illegible], future father of Morold and Yseult.

Hengist: [illegible] *I,4* – A successful mercenary, Hengist allied himself with *Horsa* to seek a kingdom to seize. They contracted with *Vortigern* and Hengist swiftly became his chief adviser, in charge of his domestic security forces and secret police. He initiated the Police State with the imprisonment and torture of the resistance leader *Eldol*, and along with Horsa orchestrated the Night of the Long Knives, eliminating effective opposition. *I,4* – Hengist continued to tighten his control over Albion through his expanding system of surveillance, militarized police, and terror. [illegible] of treason backfired by initiating the *Taliesin's* public prophesy of the regime's fall. He was slain in combat by Eldol.

Horsa: Warlord, or Eorl, of Ængals, father of *Cerdic* and *Eobessa*, son of Aelle son of Hoeroweard. ***I,3*** – A successful mercenary, he gained ascendency through his alliance with *Haengist* and *Vortigern*. In charge of the *Tower's* military colonial operations against the Sundered Tribesribes, his men were trained to kill like machines; he called them Drones, stinging for the good of the Hive. He contributed Ængalic troops to perform the massacre of the Night of the Long Knives. ***I,4*** – While collaborating with the Sax, he nonetheless plotted to turn on them after defeating the pen-Dragons, taking all of Albion for the Ængals. Impelled by his combat-madness at the Battle of the *Tower*, he saw the pen-Dragon *Uther* with his inner-eye, like the Brythons. He escaped the defeat of the Battle of the *Tower* with the remnants of his decimated force, and regrouped along the Sæxan Shoure. ***I,5*** – Having confirmed a treaty of mutual defense with *Octa's* Sax, Horsa began rebuilding his forces and raiding over the border, the launched unsuccessful invasions of Gorre and southern Albion, then opposed Uther's army of liberation. In the campaign's final battle, Horsa was killed in combat by Uther, who mounted his head upon his bedpost.

Idres: An infamous baronet, who attained considerable celebrity among the devotees of violence and Yaldabaoth cult. ***II,1*** – Idres attended the Tournament at the s'Tone-Henge and the second trial, attempting and failing to draw the s'Word herself at the latter, and eventually joining the Corporation of Barons against *Arthur*.

-king w/100 cNights: A very powerful baron based in the north of Albion, near Gore, his power such that his vassals far outnumber 100. ***II,1*** – He attempted to draw the s'Word from the s'Tone at the final trial, then joined Lot in organising armed opposition to *Arthur*, positioning himself as a strong-man against the threat of the Sæxan Shoure. He organised the robber barons into a united Corporation of Barons, which he led in the War against Arthur in alliance with the forces of *Lot*.

Lady of Lakes: A Mirrormatre magus and the ward of *Anna*, she is the transmutation of *Vivienne* pen-Dragon, born from the seed of Vivienne's death, which was planted in the mirror-lake in the dome beneath the City of Ys. ***II,1*** – Rumours speculated on her existence soon after the first reports concerning the ladies-of-lakes emerged from the wilds of Armorica. However, she made no public nor certain appearance until the Lammas day of *Arthur's* investiture, when she rose from the incoming tide surrounding Ynys Wydryn with her unrecognised acolyte, *Anna*. There, when *Lot* insulted Arthur and denied the legitimacy of his leadership, *Cador* grew enraged and called upon the Lady of Lakes to support Arthur's claim – a request that she rebuked, considering their dispute petty. Instead she reminded all assembled there that the s'Word in the s'Tone granted, at most, a provisional legitimacy, revealing that the true s'word of the pen-Dragons, Caliburn, was in her keeping and would only be given to one who had earned it. As the Lady, remaining neutral, departed under the rising tide, Arthur begged her to divulge the whereabouts of his twin, whereupon she revealed that her acolyte, at that moment being swept away by the sea, was in fact Anna – too late for them to speak on this occasion.

Lœdegrants: An ambitious southern thane; father of *Guenefaire*. ***II,1*** – During the second round of attempts, at the Solstice, he attempted and failed to draw the s'Word from the s'Tone. In the civil war following *Arthur's* investiture, he immediately offered his people's support. His land-armada of mobile gardens planted on massive wheeled carts contributed greatly to Arthur's efforts.

Lot: Scion of Gore, the child of *Rovæna* and *Uriens*. ***I,5*** – Lot was born in the wake of their parents' victory over the Barons and securing of Gorrish stability. ***II,1*** – In their adolescence, Lot won some renown as a warrior in the border-skirmishes with the Pictes and ÆngaloSæxans. In form, they took after their father the thane. Though many doubted their stability as offspring of fleshfolk and thoughtfolk, many others saw in them a harbinger of the future, and believed them to be *Arthur*; a sizeable cult arose around them, which accompanied them to the great tournament at the Stone-Henge, where *Wortimer*-Arthur drew the s'Word from the s'Tone. Lot did not participate in the contest there and kept quiet in the disputes afterward until eventually seconding their father's insistence that Lot's supporters cease their insinuations, and suggesting that more people should try the 'Word before deciding. At the second trial, they maintained his silence while his supporters argued against Arthur's cause until reined in by his mother. At the third trial, they no longer denied the claims made for them by their supporters, though they still remained silent themself. At first, their silence continued at Arthur's investiture, until the tradition of the King-as-Fool, when they used the licence granted by the rite to assail Arthur, first in mocking terms but then in deadly earnest, finally declaring that they would not take part in his investiture, nor recognise his lead.

Mark: Eldest scion of Cærnwellen, son of *Ygraine* & *Gorlois*, brother to *Ause* and half-brother to *Anna* & *Arthur*. ***I,5*** – Still an infant, Mark and his sister were taken by his mother to meet *Merlin* during his madness, where the seer prophesied a sorry fate for the child. ***II,1*** – After Ygraine's death, Mark was fostered by her loyal page *Brastias*, who served as his regent.

Constantine's assassination, he gained the ear of Vortigern, and used him to re-shape Albion into a centralised Security State on the model of Rome. With Vortigern he erected a massive panopticon-Towr by which to centralise power in a newly-militarized State, and contracted with the Sax and Ængals under *Hengist* and *Horsa* as mercenaries. When the Towr's foundations crumbled each night, Maugantius advised the ritual sacrifice of *Merlinus Ambrosius*, and that Vortigern strip Vivienne of her shared authority, imprisoning her. During the sacrificial ceremony Ambrosius-Merlinus fell into trance, foreseeing Vortigern's doom; Maugantius advised his execution, but before this could be carried out Vivienne, who had escaped confinement, appeared and cut Maugantius' throat.

Merlin/Merlinus: Albion's greatest mage and sage, an emanation of Arthur's uncle, Ambrosius-Merlinus, youngest of the pen-Dragons. Hence, the son of *Vivienne* and an unnamed Mirrorman; half-brother of *Uther* and *Vortigern* (the latter disowned); otherself to *Ambrosius*. ***I,3*** – Formerly an aspect of the dual-identity of *Merlinus-Ambrosius*, he was ushered forth as a distinct subject by Vivienne in a ritual in the Crystal Cave. Thereupon, she swathed him in a cocoon of words, where he was to sleep in this world, while living in the care of the Mirrorfolk, until the return of the pen-Dragons to Albion. ***I,4*** – Awakening on the very day on which both his mother Vivienne and his otherself Ambrosius died, Merlin made his first appearance to the people of Albion on that same day at Stonehenge, immediately after his otherself's assassination, where Uther alone recognised him. ***I,5*** – Though refusing any official post or hierarchical rank, Merlinus became Uther's closest advisor, disappearing and reappearing throughout Albion as he pleased, dedicating himself to creating the conditions for the prophesied *Arthur* to emerge. After the allied victory in Æireland, he played a competitive game with the Gælish bard *Fedelme*, and caused causing one of the Stones of the Giant's Dance to move; he conveyed the gift back to the Stone-Henge at Amesbury, a monument to Ambrosius and to the Night of the Long Knives. After the fall of the To*wr*, *Merlin* sought out *Blaise* and retired from public service for a time to serve as his apprentice. He was sought out by *Ulfin* to obtain his aid in consummating Uther's lust for *Ygraine*, and allowing himself to be tricked into believing that the request had Ygraine's and *Gorlois*' consent, provided the identity-dissolving formula with which Uther deceived Ygraine into conceiving *Arthur*. After the conception, Ygraine accused Merlinus of enabling Uther's deception, spurning his initial attempts to shirk accountability. Then, facing his responsibility, he was driven mad by his guilt and fled into the Forest Perilous, living there as a Wild Man. After three months in the Forest, he was discovered by *Brastius*, sent by Ygraine to find him and temporarily subdued by Brastias' sympathetic music; but upon reaching Tintagel, he was appalled by the crowds of people and after a bout of prophesy his madness returned and he fled back into the Forst Perilous, until he wandered into the camp of his brother's army. There Uther, terminally ill, proposed that they heal each other, and built a golden cage to contain merlin's madness; but Merlin stated that there was no undoing Ygraine's curse. He then journeyed on a ship of fools to Gæland, where he was found naked and starving in the forest by Fidelme the bard-que'en, who cared for him as an autre sister as he finally passed through his madness. Returning to Albion, Merlin devised for the dying Uther a bed which was also a war-engine, upon which he could go to combat even in his bedridden state. After the battle, Merlin brought the dying -king to Tintagel, where Ygraine was in labour. Immediately after Uther bequeathed his duties on whichever child would be first-born, he died, and Arthur and Anna were delivered. With her dying breath, denying Merlin wardship of the children, Ygraine sent Brastias in secrecy to deliver Arthur to be raised with *Ector*, and Anna in the city of Ys. Merlin refused to fill Uther's role as ruler until Arthur came of age, instead appointing *Eldol* as regent. He then called a great gathering at the Stone Henge, where he drove an enchanted S'word through an anvil into a S'tone, revealing that the one who could draw the S'word out again would be Arthur, prepared to claim his duties. ***II,1*** – After Arthur's & Anna's birth and hiding, Merlin served as Albion's regent for three years before passing the role to *Eldol*, to hold until Arthur's reappearance; he then spent another two years traveling, engaged upon mysterious pursuits, before vanishing for a decade. Some rumours had him dead, others imprisoned, others supposed him engaged in secret machinations; it was claimed he visited the *Lady of Lakes* in the grottos beneath Ys. He re-emerged at the Tournament at the s'Tone Henge, which he attended first incognito, finally revealing himself to intervene in the dispute over the legitimacy of Arthur's drawing of the s'Word from the s'Tone. He had discarded his plague-mask of old for a blank, expressionless mask of scraped white parchment. Merlin reminded the assembled folk that that this s'Word was not that which would elect Arthur as Albion's head: this was merely Uther's battle-blade, and only granted Arthur contingent leadership – only when proven worthy would Caliburn, s'Word of the pen-Dragons, reveal itself to him. Working with Eldol, he devised a compromise whereby the attempt would be repeated at the Solstice, when anybody in Albion would have the chance to make the attempt a final time. The same occured again at the second trial, and so a third and final test was set for May-day. When Arthur remained alone in drawing the s'Word, Eldol and Merlin overruled the opposition of Lot and the Barons to set his installation ceremony at Ynys Wydryn. There, when the Lady of Lakes revealed herself, he found himself both intrigued and anxious, recognising a power both intimately linked to his own, yet utterly distinct from it; he watched and listened passively to her interactions with others. When Lot and the barons refused Arthur's validity, Merlin quickly became his closest advisor, and devised the cultural, political, and magical strategies of the new provisional -king, although he refused to accept any official office, position, or honour.

morgAnor: Leader of a band who supported Lot as the potential *Arthur* prior to the drawing of the s'Word from the s'Tone; the Goreling Anor appropriated the Cærnish prefix "morg" into the Gorrish tongue. ***II,1*** – In the disputes after it was drawn, he was the most vocal advocate of Lot and opponent of Wortimer/Arthur, insisting that the whole thing was a political hoax. He was quieted by Uriens. At the second trial, Morganor himself attempted and failed to draw the s'Word, and joined Lot's forces for the war against Arthur.

morgYgraine: see **Ygraine**; the inconsistent prefix *morg-* denotes a matre of the emanant Cærnish family who has reached maturity.

Naram: a skilled glazier-thane. ***II,1*** – Naram attempted to draw the s'Word from the s'Tone in the final attempt, on a whim rather than any hope of ascendency. Naram's phalanx supported *Arthur* in the civil war against *Lot* and the barons.

Nentres: Leader of a Gorrish band. ***II,1*** – Nentres supported *Lot* as the potential *Arthur* prior to the drawing of the s'Word from the s'Tone, at the second trial loudly denounced the miracle as a hoax, until silenced by *Rovæna*, and joined Lot's forces for the war against Arthur.

Octa: Public Enforcer, then Warlord of the Sax. *I,4* – Rose to prominence for his use of public terror-strategies and spectacular shows of force to suppress protests and riots, show-trials of brythic dissidents, public torture and executions. Octa became *Hængist's* main advisor during the pen-Dragon's campaign. At the battle of Maesbeli, he betrayed Hængist when the latter called him into battle to attack *Eldol's* flank. Instead, considering the fight already lost, Octa withdrew after the defeat, using his unscathed force to assert rulership over the surviving Sax. He then returned to the City Legions, by now besieged by the pen-Dragons, who were themselves besieged by the encircling Ængal forces; at the appearance of the army of Gorre in his rear, he once again abandoned his allies, fleeing the field to save his force intact. In the wake of the Tour's fall, he thus became the de facto commander of the survivors, concentrated in the southeast along what became known as the Saxon Shoure. *I,5* – His last saxan competitors all slain, Octa took control of the remaining Sax in Albion, consolidated defense of the Saxon Shoure, and soon began raiding over the border. He paid the picte *Eopa* to assassinate Ambrosius, hoping to provoke war between the brythons and pictes, but thanks to Eldol's intervention and and Uther's restraint, no war emerged from the killing. Allying with *Hørsa's* Ængals, the two armies attacked the new Republic of Gorre, but were repulsed by Rovæna and Uriens. They then invaded southern Albion, where Octa was killed in combat by Uther, who mounted his head upon his bedpost.

Owain: Gorrish thane of Pictish extraction. ***I,5*** – In the resistance to *Octa's* and *Hørsa's* invasion, young Owain led the Gorrish war-phalanx luring the Ængalish force into *Rovæna's* trap, leading to the Gorrish victory. ***II,1*** – Owain led a force of Gorrish volunteers supporting *Arthur* in his war against *Lot's* coalition; Owain was tacitly supported by supplies, intelligence, and political immunity by *Rovæna*.

Questing Beast: A mysterious beast sporting the attributes of a lion, a leopard, a serpent, and a deer, whose call mimics that of thirty yapping dogs. It incessantly roans the *Forest Perilous*. In every generation, some *matre* or *thane* becomes enamoured with chasing it, devoting their lives to its pursuit until the Quest is gifted to one of the next generation; the beast has never been caught. ***I,5*** – Merlin, while roaming the Perilous Forest in his madness, met the Questing Beast, who taught him arcane secrets beyond the bounds of knowledge.

Riothamus: Offspring of *Ban*; scion, and then -king of Armorica after their father's death. Fluid in gender, nimble of idiom. ***I,4*** – Riothamus led the naval forces of Benoic in the expedition to liberate Albion. They secretly transported *Eldol's* fleet to the battlefield of Mæsbeli and erected pontoon bridges of *Ambrosius*' design, allowing the Cærnish forces to deliver the deathblow to the Sæxan force, sank a significant portion of the Ængalic fleet, patrolled the waterways feeding the pen-Dragon forces, and ended the massacre of Totnes by Cerdic's troops – rescued the survivors including *Vivienne*, though too late to save their father *Ban*. At the Battle of the To*w*r, they stopped the advance of *Octa's* relief force. For a season after the victory they and their fleet circulated Albion's rivers ands coasts, helping newly-freed communities to establish their peace-ways and defenses against the petty "kings. They then returned with Vivienne to Armorica, where after Ban's funeral, as -king of Armorica, they renewed the struggle against the forces of the Real assailing Benoic, with allies from Albion. ***I,5*** – Riothamus, as the ally without whose intervention Albion would remain under Sæxan domination, was widely considered the likeliest consort for Uther, and thus the prospective parent of Arthur. They destroyed a fleet of colonising barons under *Pascentricius*, supported the brythic expedition to support the Gæls, and bore the stone from the Giants' Dance back to Albion. When Uther made his attempt to wed *Ygraine* public and declared war on Cærnwellen, the betrayed Riothamus revoked Albion's alliance with Armorica, and did not participate in Uther's final campaign against the Ængalo-Sæxan invasion. However, Eldol wed *Riothamus* in the first year of his regency, repairing the rift between Albion and Armorica created by Uther.

Rovæna: Once the trascelator of the Sæx and que'en of Albion; later the que'en of Gorre; daughter of *Hængist,* consort of *Vortigern* and later *Uriens*. ***I,3*** – Hængist's official transcelator, she was secretly opposed to her people's patriarchal rule; as her status demanded, she did not speak her own words from the day of her initiation until her wedding-night. She was the medium for all of her father's interactions with *Vortigern* until, on the arrangement of Hængist, she married the -King. She attempted to convince Vortigern to lead Albion away from its patriarchal path toward fascism, but he refused. She then arranged a parlay to that purpose between the powers of the To*w*r and the folk gathered around

Taliesin at Avebury. When Hængist and *Hørsa* massacred those gathered there in the Night of the Long Knives, Rovæna, aghast, saved *Eldol's* life by cutting his bonds to let him escape; her father beat her, put her under guard, and returned her to the Towr as a prisoner. ***I,4*** – Kept alive thanks to her unique ability to translate the brythic language, she was kept kept under close watch and suspicion. She regularly visited Taliesin, plotting in sympathy with him against her father's regime. A trap was set for her, whereby the rebel Taliesin's life would be placed in her hands in a public ceremony, and her clemency taken as proof of her own treason. Spotting the trap, and after failing to persuade him recant, she finally agreed to the latter's death, then performed a ritual dance of divorce from Vortigern When Taliesin was beheaded, his full power was released against the Towr, in the form of a prophesy uttered by his magically floating head. Warned of Hørsa's plan to assassinate her, she escaped to Gorre, where she renounced her Sæxan citizenship and worked with *Blaise* to promote desertion among the Sæx and their integration into Albion, eventually re-wedding to *Uriens*, and thus becoming the Matron of Gore. They launched a campaign coordinated with that of the pen-Dragons, ambushing and destroying the Sæxan army of *Wippid*, then joining the pen-Dragons on the second day of the Battle of the Towr. After the victory she and Uriens returned to Gorre to un-construct the Wall, and strengthen the bonds of the new society. ***I,5*** – Rovæna and Uriens forced the Barons and remaining Sæx out of Gorre, after which they were delivered of the child *Lot*, and repulsed an Ængalo-Sæxan invasion on their own, having cancelled their alliance with Albion in response to Uther's war in Cærnwellen. ***II,1*** – In order to evaluate the dispute over the s'Word&s'Tone, Rovæna attended the second trial, where she was disturbed about the cult-like support gathering around her son Lot, and curbed his most vocal lackeys in the following debates. She and Uriens led the formal retinue from Gorre to *Arthur's* investiture festival on Lammas, and when Lot finally declared his open opposition to Arthur, Rovæna ended up declaring neutrality but reluctantly siding against her son behind the scenes, suspicious of the zealotry he inspired, and despite her consort's support for Lot, thus precipitating a crisis in Gorre as its citizens supported one or the other party, or else maintained neutrality.

Sanam: Prominent brython, a refugee from the region of Guinntuic, now part of the Sæxan Shoure. ***II,1*** – Greatly demoralised by Albion's troubles in the years after Uther's death, present at the drawing of the s'Word from the s'Tone. At the second trial, they made the attempt themselves, and failed. Sanam's phalanx supported Arthur in the civil war against Lot and the barons.

Taliesin's Head: ***I,4*** – Initially the head of the Bard *Taliesin*, when released from his body it leapt into the air, uttering the prophesy of the To*w*r's fall and the future manifestation of *Arthur*. After the pen-Dragon liberation, Taliesin's head, magically re-animated, was placed atop the May-Pole at the Stone Henge, where it sang songs of joy and death to terrify the distant enemies along the Sæxan Shoure. ***I,5*** – On the first birth-day of Anna and Arthur, Taliesin's head sang in celebration before the setting of the S'word in the S'tone. ***II,1*** – At the great Tournament at the s'Tone Henge, Taliesin's head sang the dance to which the assembled citizens danced on the first day, and announced the various contests and games on the second day. It watched Wortimer/Arthur draw the s'Word from the s'Tone, and merrily championed him in the ensuing contents, ridiculing the failed contestants for their attempts on all occasions.

Talorc: An ambitious pictish chieftain. ***II,1*** – Finding his chances for advancement unlikely among the pictes, Talorc allied himself with Lot's armies in the war against Arthur.

Uriens of Gorre: Co-founder of the Republic of Gorre. ***I,4*** – Uriens rose to prominence as a leader in the Pictic rebellion against the Ængals. Forging an alliance that spanned both sides of the Wall and incorporated not only Pictes but disgruntled Brythons, Thoughtfolk, and Ængalic deserters, he then made contact with *Blaise* and secured an alliance with the pen-Dragons. He gave safe-haven to *Rovæna*, eventually wedding her. Together they launched a campaign coordinated with that of the pen-Dragons, ambushing and destroying the army of *Wippid*, then joining the pen-Dragons on the second day of the Battle of the To*w*r. After the victory he and Rovæna returned to Gore to strengthen the bonds of the new society. ***I,5*** – Uriens and Rovæna forced the Barons and remaining Sæx out of Gorre in a bitter campaign, after which they were delivered of the child *Lot*, and repulsed an Ængalo-Sæxan invasion on their own, having cancelled their alliance with Albion in response to Uther's war in Cærnwellen. ***II,1*** – In form, Urien's son Lot took after their father the thane, and many believing the boy to be *Arthur*, a sizeable cult arose around him, whom Uriens accompanied to support him at the great tournament at the Stone-Henge, where Wortimer-Arthur drew the s'Word from the s'Tone. Uriens curbed the other gorelyngs' slander of Wortimer and advocacy of his son, but did not officially support Wortimer either. He and Rovæna led the formal retinue from Gorre to Arthur's investiture festival on Lammas, and when Lot finally declared his open opposition to Arthur, Uriens ended up reluctantly siding with his son, despite his consort's support for the pen-Dragon, thus precipitating a crisis in Gorre as its citizens supported one or the other party, or else maintained neutrality.

Uther: deceased pen-Dragon, the father of *Arthur*; son of *Vivienne* and *Constantine*, brother of *Ambrosius-Merlinus* and *Vortigern* (the former by half, the latter disowned). ***I,1*** – Charged as a child, upon his father's death, with acting as the S'word of Albion, wielding its combined will upon the world with honour. ***I,2*** – A stalwart youth, hot-tempered, honest, earthy, direct, preternaturally gifted; imprisoned along with his mother by Vortigern, he fought alongside her, *Eldol*, and others, rescuing Ambrosius-Merlinus and escaping. ***I,3*** – Uther fled with Vivienne and *Ambrosius* to Armorica, where he began training for war with *Ban's* forces, having declared vengeance upon Vortigern. ***I,4*** – though still a child, he acquired a reputation for military skill fighting the Francks, Sæx, and Danes. He led the primary military force in the campaign to liberate Albion, killing the sæxan spylord *Æsc* and breaking his shield-wall at the battle of Mæsbeli. After the To*w*r's fall, his warbands pursued the remaining forces to the coastal territory thenceforth known as the Sæxan Shoure. ***I,5*** – Uther became -king after Ambrosius' murder, personally responding to the renewed Sæxan threat as his comrades continued the projects begun by themselves and Ambrosius. Convinced by the bard *Fedelme* to aid the Gæls in their struggle against colonising robber-barons, Uther crossed to Gæland where he allied with *Gilloman* to defeat *Pascentricius*. After his return to Albion, lacking the counsel of Merlinus who had departed to study under *Blaise*, Uther pressed Ygraine to renounce *Gorlois*, become his primary consort, and bear the future *Arthur* despite her depleted powers. When she refused, offering him only a second-consortship without offspring, he declared Cærnwellen in rebellion, and called Albion to arms against it, though many refused the call. Having sent *Ulfin* to implore Merlin's aid in fulfilling the -king's lust, Uther invaded Cærnwellen and besieged the twin tors of the Cast'le Tintagel and Cast,le Terrible, held by Ygraine and Gorlois respectively. When Ulfin returned with Merlin's formula which dissolved the distinctions and blend the identities of matres and thanes, Uther used it to assume Gorlois' form, and deceived Ygraine in order to conceive Arthur. Afterward, aghast and outraged at Uther's betrayal, Ygraine cursed him, and declared that Arthur and Anna should never leave her womb until their father lie dead. Soon, he returned to the Sæxan Shoure to defend against a new invasion. There, while preparing his forces, he fell terminally ill. Merlin, stricken mad by his guilt for the role he had played in the deception of Ygraine, wandered into Uther's camp out of the Forest Perilous. Uther proposed that they heal each other, and built a golden cage to contain merlin's madness; but Merlin stated that there was no undoing Ygraine's curse, and Uther released him. In the spring, having alienated his former allies in Gorre and Benoic as well as many of his own people such as Eldol, Uther's illness deepened as his forces struggled with the invasion of *Horsa* and Octa. Returning after passing through his madness, Merlin devised for Uther a bed which was also a war-engine, upon which he could go to combat even in his bedridden state. He rode into his final battle upon this chariot-cot, wreaking great violence on the enemy, killing both Octa and Hørsa, and spiking their heads upon his bedposts as the sæxængalic shield-walls collapsed & the victory fell to to Albion. Merlin brought the dying -king to Tintagel, where Ygraine was in labour. Immediately after Uther bequeathed his duties on whichever child would be first-born, he died, never seeing his children, Ygraine's curse fulfilled.

[illegible]

[illegible]

even greater youth, alone in his father's tomb, Vortigern expressed fear and uncertainty regarding his new duties; in reaching out to ritually don Wyrmwhit, the sacred Helm, he dropped it to the ground three times – a dire omen for his stewardship. He fainted in terror, and upon waking was privy to Vivienne's secret confession about Ambrosius-Merlinus' patrimony. *I,2* – Weak and overwhelmed, Vortigern fell under the sway of *Maugantius*, and was led by him to build a massive panopticon *Towr* by which to centralise power in a newly-militarized State. When the *Towr*'s foundations crumbled each night, Maugantius advised the ritual sacrifice of a Mirrorman's son; Vortigern betrayed his brother and offered him for sacrifice, imprisoning Vivienne and Uther. During the ceremony Ambrosius-Merlinus fell into a prophetic trance, foreseeing Vortigern's doom. His family, who had disowned him, escaped after killing Maugantius. *I,3* – In order to secure his authority in the face of brewing rebellion at home and by Vivienne in Armorica, Vortigern contracted the Sæx and Ængals under *Hængist* and *Hørsa* as mercenaries. Now under Hængist's influence, he introduced Property and class into brythic society and became the figurehead for a hyper-nationalist, militaristic surveillance state. He married *Rowena* but rejected her plea to lead Albion away from its patriarchal path toward fascism. *I,4* – After Rowena's banishment he became yet more isolated, no longer able to communicate effectively with his Sæx wardens and unsafe among his own people. During the battle of the Towr, he was abandoned by most of his last brythic supporters, including many of his mnemnomancers, leaving him sickly and verging on dissipation-death. He watched the battle alone from his Towr on high; as the City walls fell to the pen-Dragons, a flame-bolt from one of *Ambrosius*' war-engines struck the Towr and lit it aflame. Trapped inside, Vortigern burned to death therein.

Wihtgar: Ængalic warlord, *Hørsa's* treasurer and steward. ***I,4*** – Supplanted *Wlencing* as *Hørsa's* closest advisor in the City of Legions after Wlencing's disgrace. ***II,1*** – After the fall of the Towr regime, Wihtgar became *Cerdic's* main rival as the latter rose to control of the Ængalo-Sæxan confederation.

Wortimer / Wort: see **Arthur**.

Ygraine/morgYgraine: Steward-Matre and leader of Cærnwellen; the mother of *Arthur* and *Anna* by Uther; wed to *Gorlois*, her primary consort, and by her the mother of *Ause* and *Mark*. ***I,4*** – Having evaded by distance the full surveillance of the Sæx, Cærnwellen became a centre of Albion's resistence. Ygraine coordinated with *Ambrosius* via *Blaise* to stage an uprising simultaneous with their invasion. She quickly assembled an army of brythic refugees which joined the pen-Dragons. She met *Uther*, and between them complicated and unspoken impressions passed. She commanded her own war-troupe at the battles of Maesbeli and of the Towr. ***I,5*** – After the fall of Towr, Ygraine led the phalanx of pen-Sans, accompanied by Gorlois, circulating the westcountry spreading nuturemancy. When the -king left to campaign in Æireland, Ygraine was named temporary regent in his absence. Over the next three years, Uther's attraction to her grew to madness, until finally he pressed Ygraine to

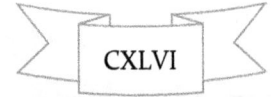

renounce Gorlois, become his primary consort, and bear the future Arthur despite her depleted powers. When she refused, offering him only a second-consortship without offspring, the -king declared Cærnwellen in rebellion, and called Albion to arms against it, though many refused the call. Splitting their forces between two impregnable hill-forts, Ygraine was fortified at the Cast'le Tintagel, while Gorlois held its sister-fort, the Cast'le Terrible; both were besieged by Uther's forces. Uther used an identity-dissolving formula from *Merlinus* to assume Gorlois' form, and deceived Ygraine in order to conceive Arthur. At the last moment, she realised Uther's true identity, and sacrificed most of her remaining life-force to assure Arthur's healthy development. But at the moment of Arthur's conception, she realised Uther's deception and violation; Ygraine withheld some part of herself from Arthur's seed, refusing the violence of Uther's inheritance, dividing and diverting the surge of generation, and in the space of this withdrawal the seed of Anna was planted. Afterward, aghast and outraged at Uther's betrayal, Ygraine cursed him, and declared that Arthur and Anna should never leave her womb until their father lie dead. She also castigated *Merlinus* for his role, giving the lie to his excuses and apologies, until he was driven mad by his guilt. Nonetheless, after the first phase of his madness Ygraine, took pity on him, and sent *Brastias* to lure the magician back to society by means of his enchanting music. Subdued by Brastias' sympathetic music, Merlinus returned and met Ygraine and her children Mark and Ause, prophesying on each; but upon reaching Tintagel, he was appalled by the crowds of people, his madness returned, and he ran off again. When the Ængals and Sæx invaded in the Spring, she kept her curse upon Uther's person, but nonetheless sent a Cærnish war-phalanx under *Brastias* to aid in Albion's defence. She went into labour at precisely the moment that Uther joined in his final battle, a labour which lasted a week while Merlin brought the dying -king to Tintagel. Immediately after Uther bequeathed his duties on whichever child would be first-born, he died, and Arthur and Anna were delivered. With her dying breath, Ygraine sent Brastias in secrecy to deliver Arthur to be raised with *Ector*, and Anna to a certain Lady he would meet in the city of Ys.

Appendix III:

Glossary

of Albion's Society and Places

Æireland: The *Ængalic* colony in *Gœland.*

Ængals: People given over to the *Real*, characterized by hate refined, turned cold and hard like metal.

Albion: A land of double-life, the material and the abstract cleaved together, in which the *Real* lives in deference and wonderment of Thought; inhabited by *brythons*, *matres*, and *thanes*.

Albrithon/Albrithionic: A term that emerged during the interregnum between Uther's and Arthur's epochs, to describe the merged social identity of the bythons, thanes & matres. Sometimes used to distinguish from Ængalised brythons who no longer live amongst the thoughtfolk; likewise united Albrithon, vs. Albion and brython distinct.

Amesbury: Traditional heart of Albion: a place of barrows, menhirs, sacred circles, springs and groves.

Armorica: An outpost of *Albion* in the realm of the *Real*, across the *Sea*. Technically the community's conceptual aspect while *Benoic* represents its material aspect (as with Albion and *Brythain*), though in practice Armorica and Benoic are often employed interchangeably.

Aristocrat: see **Baron.**

Army: A *phalanx* gathered temporarily, usually to achieve a collective purpose or to compete with other armies in the creation of beauty and culture; however, among the *Romans*, *Sœx*, *Ængals*, and sometimes *Albion* and the *Sundered Tribes*, armies are often employed for mass political murder.

Avalon: Land of Abstraction, thought, potential, love; *Albion's* lovely mirror, casting light upon it; inhabited by the *Mirrorpeople*.

Avebury: Consecrated circle of giant Standing Stones at *Amesbury*, site of *Albion's* communal rites, birthing-ground of the *pen-Dragons*, and containing the great Barrow which is the pen-Dragons' ancestral tomb.

Baron: (aka Aristocrat, Noble, Lord, Noble, King, etc.) A *brython* who, as a reward for collaborating with occupying forces or, later, through sheer threat of violence, has been granted exclusive rights of private Property which are leveraged to exert power over the surrounding communities. Only males are considered candidates for No-bility, and their power passes along thet male line regardless of the inheritor's character or skill. After the fall of the *Towr*, ex-*œngals* and ex-*sœx* also became barons, and perpetuated their petty states by means of tyranny, violence, extortion, and custom. Often called *Robber-Barons*, since they live off others' stolen labour.

Benoic: An outpost of *Albion* in the realm of the *Real*, across the *Sea*. Technically the community's material or Real aspect while *Armorica* represents its abstract aspect, as with *Brythain* and Albion, though in practice "Armorica" and "Benoic" are often employed interchangeably. Engaged in constant defensive warfare against encroaching *Sœx* and *Frœncks*.

Brythain: That part of *Albion* belonging to the world that Is, partaking of the *Real*.

Brython: An embodied citizen of *Albion*, who is coincident with a material anatomy.

Cærleon: the *pen-Dragons*' home *phalanx*, with whom in peaceful times they roamed *Albion* in continual visitation; during the occupation of the *Towr*, its *phalanstery* was converted to an immobile *city* of stone, and re-named the *City of Legions*.

Cærnwellen / Cærnwallen: Southwesternmost region of *Albion*, keeping close sisterly ties with *Armorica*.

Caliburn: Ceremonial S'word of *Albion*, kept by the *pen-Dragons*.

Cenacle: A social unit smaller than a phalanstery, united by a common affinity or shared passion which constitutes the common lodestone of the group's identity, activity, and relations.

City: A *phalanx* that has been forced to remain forever a single place, to petrify its form and layout, and to standardize its population.

City of Legions: Name given to *Cærleon* by the government of the *Towr*, after its conversion into an immobile city of stone. When liberated by the *pen-Dragons*, the stone buildings were razed and the mobile phalanstery restored, thus cutting the City of Legions from Cærleon's body politic like a cancer.

The Cloud: A film of corruption released in the burning of the *Towr*, which ever afterward pervades the atmosphere of *Albion*, sometimes oppressively, sometimes imperceptibly. It causes drought and famine in the material world, corruption and short-sightedness in the thought world.

The Crystal Cave: A womb of reflections, water and crystal and air, wherein magical ~~birthings~~ and deaths may take place miraculously; twin-crucible of the subterranean cave-lake under *Ys*.

Dænes: A ship-faring people who live upon the *Sea of the Real*, raiding along its borders.

Dargwythievoder: Ceremonial Shield of *Albion*, kept by the *pen-Dragons*.

Devon/Dumnonia: Southwestern region, eastward of *Cærnwellen*; home to the river Dart and the great moors. Devon to the *Brythons*, Dumnonia to the *Thoughtfolk*, in practice both names are often used interchangeably. Region where the *pen-Dragon* expedition to liberate Albion landed.

Drone: *Ængalic* soldiers, trained to kill like machines: devoid of ethical, emotional, or technological constraints.

Eørl: Official title of the overlord of the *Ængals*.

Exeter: A *phalanx* calcified as a *City* under the *Towr's* regime, in *Albion's* south, on what was after known as the River Exe, and a major military and administrative centre for the occupying forces of the occupying *Sæx*.

Forest Perilous: A dangerous, primeval dream-place of unchartable, shifting paths and obscure shadow, given over to the play of chance; an ungoverned and ungovernable world of ever-imminent adventure – the womb, home, and refuge of both wonderment and horror. The Forest Perilous extends through much of *Albion*; before the *Romans* came, it is said to have encompassed the Island completely.

Francks (also *Frænks*, etc.): A people given over to the *Real*, perpetually invading *Benoic*.

Gæland: Island inhabited by the *Gæls*; see also *Æireland*.

Gæls: One of the *Sundered Tribes*, inhabiting an island neighbouring *Albion*. At war with Albion since the early days of Maugantius' tenure as border-ward, when he began provoking them and developing a subtle propaganda campaign against them within Albion.

Gastromancer: One dedicated to the cultivation and proliferation of gastronomy, food, nourishing drink, and pleasures relating to the comfort of the body.

The Giants' Dance: A ring of gargantuan menhirs near *Killaire*, sacred to the *Gæls*; it is said that the stones are the calcified bodies of the giant entities that preceded the flesh-people and the *thought-people* upon the world. In those days, they had danced in an endless ring outside of time, their arms linked. They were turned to stone by the first rain, caused by the archon Lugh; over the succeeding millennia, their forms have been eroded away by the succeeding rains.

Glevum: Site of a massacre in which *Ængals* under Cerdic killed Ban and roughly half of the peacephalanx of *Totnes* led by Vivienne, before the survivors' rescue by Riothamus' fleet.

Gore / Gorre: Originally a region occupied by the *Pictes* and split by the Wall of Hadrian, during the *Ængalic* occupation it became a giant refugee camp occupied by *Pictes*, *Brythons*, *Thoughtfolk*, and Ængalic and *Sæxan* deserters. The rebel leader Uriens united Gorre into a hyper-fluid, pluralistic hybrid society in revolt against the *Towr's* rule.

Killaire: Site sacred to the *Gæls*, a place of barrows, menhirs, sacred circles, springs and groves, including the *Giants' Dance*.

-king (*see also* ***que'en***): *Thane* who, emanating from the community of a *phalanx*, focuses its coordinated action, and represents it in the management of *Albion*. A male executive pen-Dragon is -king of Albion in their capacity as conduit-for-action.

"king or **King**: Aristocratic position which is a distortion of the function of *-kings*, introduced by the *Sæx* – a male *brython* who, by means of coercion, coordinates the citizens under his control for the benefit of himself, his blood-family, and his economic, political and military supporters. Aristocratic/Baronic governance is patriarchal, and does not tolerate feminine leadership.

Law: That which neither joy, nor justice, nor love may withstand or sway.

Lord: see **Baron**.

Mæsbeli: Battle in which the combined forced of the *pen-Dragons*, *Armorica*, *Cœrnwellen*, and *Albion* in revolt destroyed the main force of the *Sæx*. Hængist was slain in combat by Eldol while Octa's reserve forces abandoned the main army and fled east to regroup and retain control over Sæx-held territory.

Matre: A female, or predominantly feminine *Thoughtperson*.

Mirrorpeople / Mirrorfolk: Un-anchored subjects without images of themselves; inhabitants of *Avalon* who borrow images of *Thoughtpeople* or embodied people in order to interact with them; known to *Romans* as dæmons, to the *Ængals* as the Fay or fairies.

Mnemnomancer: A brython whose vocation is to maintain the health, happiness, and social circulation of large numbers of *Thoughtfolk*, by means of intensive meditation and intentional conversation. Called "Thane Priests" by the *Sæx*.

Night of the Long Knives: Massacre in which the *Sæx* took advantage of an alleged peace conference at *the Stone Henge* to slaughter thousands of unarmed thanes, matres, and brythons; Eldol was the sole survivor, having fought his way out with a weapon wrested from an attacker.

Nurturemancer: One whose vocation is the accelerated fostering of growth, generosity, development, and joy in the communities they inhabit.

Peace-Phalanx: Any *phalanx* oriented in unitary fashion toward the application of empathetic force in the achievement of a particular goal. Traditionally in *Albion*, every *war-phalanx* must be linked with two peace-phalanxes when conflict is unavoidable, but the forces of the *Towr* ignored this convention, the *Sæx* secret police distorting the function of the Peace-Phalanx into Propaganda.

pen-Dragon: *Matre* or *Thane* evoked and given life by the communal will of *Albion's* people, to direct the multiplicity of their Thought in accordance to their collective desires; at any time there should be two *pen-Dragons* ascendent (a *matre* and a *thane*) and two descendent (their children), but in recent centuries this order has been disrupted.

Phalanstery: The material element of the *Phalanx*, as distinct from the community itself; sometimes, an immobile farm whose occupants rotate.

Phalanx: A traveling city of *Albion*, whose shape and population continuously transmute.

Pictes: One of the *Sundered Tribes*, inhabiting the northern part of *Brythain*. Currently subject to a social disease whereby those inflicted praise all Pain, and until the advent of *Gorre*, at war with *Albion* since the early days of Maugantius' tenure as border-ward, when he began expanding brythic settlements forcibly into Pictish territory.

que'en (*see also* ***-king***): *Matre* who, emanating from the community of a *phalanx*, focuses its coordinated action, and represents it in the management of *Albion*. A female executive pen-Dragon is -que'en of Albion in their capacity as conduit-for-action.

Questing Beast: See Appendix II, Dramatis Personae.

Rhongomyniad: Ceremonial Spear of *Albion*, kept by the *pen-Dragons*.

The Real: A force and a place wherein Thought loses all power but shadow; the reign of Necessity, Limit, Matter, What-is, Voidless-Death.

Robber Barons: see **Barons**

Rome: Empire of Positivism; Rule of implacable Law, of Domination, of Utility, of Techné divorced from Ethics; Coloniser, Homogenizer, Bureaucratizer, avatar of Regulated Violence. Abjection before the Real, wearing the iron mask of Mastery. Once hegemonic in *Albion*, its spears have been absent there for several generations; yet even in its decay it continues to wreak its violence on the colonies it has poisoned.

Sæx (also *Sais*): People given over to the *Real*, characterized by love of *Law*, bloodlust trained in Power's service. According to some, one of the *Sundered Tribes*, corrupted by the *Romans* and subject to a social disease whereby those inflicted are devoted now to the deities of Death.

Sæxan Shoure: Territory along *Albion's* southeastern coast still held by the *Sæx* and *Ængals* after Vortigern's fall.

Sea of the Real: *Albion's* rim, the horizon of Living Thought, the magic circle, beyond which the *Real* dominates and enslaves Thought, exterminating what-should-be.

Shaman: A *thane*, *matre*, or occasionally a *brython* trained for consort with *Avalon*.

The Stone Henge: An ancient circle of menhirs near *Amesbury*, a magical site which hosts many of *Albion's* sacred and civic gatherings, festivals, and rites.

Sundered Tribes: The *Gæls*, the *Pictes*, and according to some the *Sæx*. Once inseparable from the *Brythons*, these tribes evaded *Roman* rule (though not the Roman poison) and were made Other by the Romans, by means of walls and roads and tariffs; henceforth foreign to the ways of *Albion*, they were at war with Albion from the days of Maugantius' tenure as border-ward until Ambrosius and Uther forged peace with them.

Supplemental Spouse/Wedlock: In the oft-polygamous society of *Albion*, a spouse with whom mutual responsibilities are less imperative, subsumed into the primary wedlocks of each. Such unions remain provisional and may not be permanent; offspring from secondary wedlock is taboo. When wedlocked thanes and matres do not die together with their primary spouse, secondary liaisons may bloom into primary wedlock.

Sword / S'word: Swords are steel, and will slice the flesh; S'words slice the will, and steal it from the flesh.

Thane: A male, or predominantly masculine *Thoughtperson*.

Thane-Priest: Sæxan slang for *Mnemnomancer*.

Thoughtchamber: A pavilion, room, or other space strewn with meditative runes and figures, in which *thanes* and *matres* may carry on more direct or precise or wholebodied consort with brythons.

Thoughtpeople / Thoughtfolk: Citizens of Avalon who are not co-incident with fleshly bodies – individuated archetypes, projections, tulpas. They are evoked within the communal thought of the brythons, and live their lives within the nerve-space that fuses Albion to Avalon, consciousness to empathy.

Tintagel Cast'le: The place of Arthur's & Anna's conception and birth, a nearly impregnable hill-fort and phalanstery-hub on *Cærnwellen's* coast; sister-tor of *Terrible Cast,le*.

Terrible Cast,le: A nearly impregnable hill-fort and phalanstery-hub on *Cærnwellen's* coast; sister-tor of *Terrible Cast,le*.

Totnes: A phalanx oriented toward arts, learning, and challenge, calcified as a Town under the *Towr's* regime upon the River Dart in Devon. It was the landing-place of the *pen-Dragons* in the expedition to liberate *Albion*, and was adopted as home-tribe by Vivienne after it was freed from its stone-walls. As such it participated in the campaign as a *peace-phalanx* and facilitated the cultural renewal of Albion against the Towr's hegemony.

the Towr: A monstrous tower upon a tor in the centre of the *City of Legions*, built at Vortigern's direction of stone, wood, and concretised thought: the hub of the Sæxan panopticon, the pinnacle of Vortiguern's hegemony, a vast Mill of thought where Fascism was manufactured. It was destroyed by Ambrosius and Uther, but the smoke from its demise formed *the Cloud*.

Wall: Wall of stone first built by Hadrian of the *Romans*, which created and maintained a state of otherment between the peoples of *Albion*, henceforth designated as *Brythons* and *Pictes*. Manned by the Roman army and later by brythic forces under the control of *Maugantius*, until the creation of the Republic of *Gorre*, which demilitarised it until the chaos following the assassination of *Uther pen-Dragon*, and again after the advent of *Arthur*.

War-Phalanx: A *phalanx*-community oriented in unitary fashion toward the application of offensive or defensive violence. Called by Sæx an "army".

Wyrmwiht: Sacred symbolic Helm of Albion, which crowns the pen-Dragon chosen to head their people.

Yaldabaoth: Monotheistic deity of Assimilation and Unicity, brought to the Isle of Albion by the Ængalic priest Colgrimliche and widely spread among the Ængalo-Sæxans, and even among some of the flesh-clothed brythons. His is a cult of conquest and consumption unquenchable, antithesis to the Camelot of Arthur and Anna.

Ynys Wydryn: Also known as the Isle of Glass. Sacred site of Albion, the site of Councils, Carnivals, and Investitures of the pen-Dragons. It is a hill in the centre of a vast floodplain on Albion's westward coast, which at high tide becomes an island connected to land by one narrow causeway.

Ys: Capital city of *Armorica*, an embattled bastion of the endangered learning and culture of *Albion*, a massive amalgamation of library, city, symposium, labyrinth, thought-palace, and fortress decorated with mosaics, paintings and carvings. Built on an isthmus jutting from Armorica into the *Sea of the Real*, it becomes an island at high tide. Underneath its foundations lay a magical cave housing an enchanted lake, whose water kills thoughtfolk, but whose death-magic was mastered by Vivienne, who drank of it as she died to be re-conceived as the Lady of Lakes.

Appendix IV

Map of Albion & its Neighbouregions

1– Ynys Wydryn

2– the s'Tone-Henge

3– Amesbury

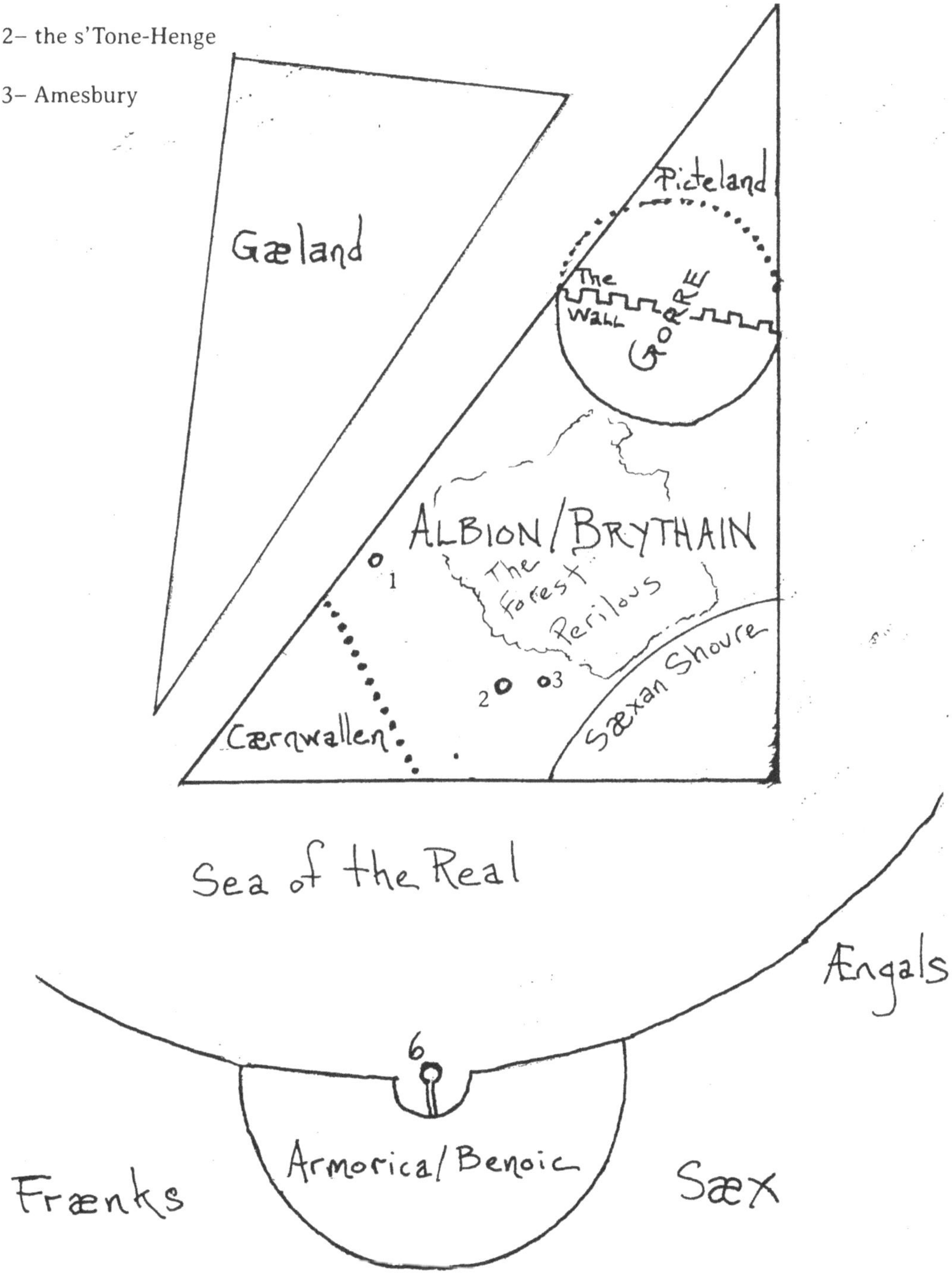

Appendix V
A Palimpsest of Sources

Patchen's *Journal of Albion Moonlight,*
The Once and Future King by T.H. White,
Le Morte d'Arthur of Malory,
Species of Abandoned Light by Jake Berry,
Chaucer's Tales of Canterbury,
Eco's *Prague Cemetery,*
The *Teatro Grottesco* of Ligotti,
The Pope's Mustard-Maker of Jarry
  and his *Days & Nights* too,
David Beris Edwards' *Ballyhoo,*
Fourier's *Four Movements,*
The Three Steles of Seth,
Mysteries of Forgotten Worlds by Helsem,
Argüelles' *Translation to Heaven,*
Dune by Frank Herbert,
The Alliterative *Death of King Arthur,*
Boorman's *Excalibur,*
The Nonsense of Edward Lear,
Bennett's *Mailer leaves Ham,*
'The Return' & others by Algernon Blackwood
Th'amulet poems of Edward Sanders,
The pwoermds of Huth & aND,
Shel Silverstein's *A Light in the Attic,*
Fatty Arbunkle's slapstick,
The Vorrh of Brian Catling,
Tolkien's Fellowship of the Ring,
The verse of Lewis Carroll,
Monmouth's *Historia Regum Britanniae,*
And too the *Jerusalem* and *Milton* of Blake,
The Four Movements of Fourier,
Albert-Birot's *Grabinoulor,*
Vaudeville of Abbot and Costello

The *Unforbiddens* of John Crouse,
Dostoevski's *Notes from the Underground,*
Crowley's *Book of Thoth,*
The *Testament* of poor Villon,
Byron's *Don Juan,*
The *Brut* of Layamon,
Cornwell's *Enemy of God,*
The Mabinogion,
The Hypostasis of the Archons,
Zimmer-Bradley's Mists of Avalon,
The *Don Quixote* of Cervantes,
Schreber's *Memoirs of my Nervous Illness*
The Anglo-Saxon Chronicles,
The Songs of Son-Jara, else-spelld Sunjata,
Rabelais' *Gargantua,*
& at last the *Popol Vuh,*

Appendix VI:
Afterword

by Jim Leftwich

prophememorcy = b*read*knife
Read = attend and interpret.
Read = look and think.
Listen to what you see.

prophememorcy
Come in from the cold, into the house of the book, the house that Poem built. It is as you read this 2024 at the earliest. Global warming will in time freeze millions of us to death.

prophememorcy
Rubbing two letters together
Rubbing two morphemes two phonemes together
Rubbing two syllables together
Rubbing two words together
Will start a fire
The book already burning shall be neither banned nor burned.

prophememorcy
There is a narrative, and it moves in at least two directions, simultaneously, sequentially, and sometimes some of it moves backwards.

Parse the diagonal overprintings.
A gain, which is a loss, which together are a gain.

Make it next, as good as new.

prophememorcy
doomingle
mingle what, or with what
in camelot citee of poetry

doomd b*read*knife
read the bread read the
knife read the breadknife
if doomed remains doomed
may it be so within the nourishment
and the nourishing

prophememorcy
This myth of Arthur and of Author is writing against itself in its extreme of generative mutagenesis.

As we recall, so shall we become.
Remember the old prophecies, when the old prophecies are new memories.

Arthur Dies
First Chronicle:
Heirs Of Constantine

by Olchar E. Lindsann

VOLUME I – published March 2015

VOLUME II – published August 2017

VOLUME III – published July 2018

VOLUME IV – published January 2021

VOLUME V – published March 2022

www.ingramcontent.com/pod-product-compliance
Lightning Source LLC
Chambersburg PA
CBHW080402170426
43193CB00016B/2788
9781938521997